THE COM WIT & WHIMSEY

" a view of life from the safety of the Cotswolds"

for Mrs. Watkins
Mike Rafferty

by
Mike Rafferty

Published by Mike Rafferty
ISBN 978-0-9525041-2-2
Printed by Quorum Printing Services Ltd, Cheltenham
Copies available from your bookseller or from Mike Rafferty:
mike_and_les@btinternet.com
© Mike Rafferty 2011

The COMPLETE WIT & WHIMSEY

FOREWORD

A few years ago, to assist the local blind club who had had a speaker cancellation at the last minute, I was asked to read some poems from my two "Wit & Whimsey" books. I was only too happy to plug this gap, and I soon found myself giving readings to many other blind clubs. In response to a request from these clubs, I recorded a CD of poems, and was delighted when this was selected by the RNIB for their Talking Books service.

Then the whole recital business escalated, as I was invited to clubs of every conceivable type over a wide area of the West of England whose meetings feature a speaker. I've enjoyed every minute of these recitals, and one feature common to most is the requests I receive to reprint the "Wit & Whimsey" books of the 1990's, both of which quickly sold out. Thinking things over, I decided that straight reprints would fall far short of what I could now offer.

To begin with, there was the large body of work I've written subsequently, some of which features in my recitals, but which has so far eluded publication. And as the "Wit & Whimsey" books were produced specifically as vehicles for humorous verse and by design did not contain any of the (for want of a better word) "serious" poems I have written over the years, a third, more comprehensive book would be the opportunity to include those. Moreover, those two earlier books contained no more than a smattering of the many limericks I have churned out over several decades, and I could really go to town with them this time. So, here we are – something for everyone, I trust. You will find here the full range from the absurd to the thought-provoking, the nostalgic to the hilarious.

I have organised the poems into four groupings, the first three of which bring the lighter side of my poetry together. First come the longer tales in verse, some based on fairy or bible stories, others just stories plucked from life. Next we have the shorter stories and other poems in lighter vein. These are followed by the limericks and similar shorties – almost 130 of them. To end with, there are the more serious poems. So please get stuck in and enjoy all parts of this book. I firmly believe that whatever else poetry should do, it should at least entertain or stimulate. It should not exist to be puzzled over. It should be accessible. Finally, I make no apology for giving a brief introduction to most of my poems. This contextual feature is generally missing from so many collected works and the reader is perhaps the poorer for its absence. A brief introduction to a poem invites an intimacy between poet and reader and can, I believe, considerably enhance enjoyment.

Mike Rafferty
Winchcombe, May 2011

CONTENTS

Foreword 2

List of Contents 3

Part 1 A Few Stories and Ballads

Re Creation 7
Adam's Apple. 8
Rain Stopped Play. 10
God Loves Atheists. Too. 14
A Bit of Rough 15
The Bottom Line 16
It's Love (in so many words) 18
Sins of Commission (a modern barrack-room ballad) 20
A Breakfast Serial (in twenty servings) 23
The French Connection 28
When Charlie Cut the Cable 30
To Boldly Return 32
A Whole New Ball Game 34
The Frog Prince. 38
The King's Incredible Lightweight Robes 41
Fosdyke of the FCO 45
Talking Shop 49

Part 2 In Lightest Vein

Crush. 53
The British Style. 54
Paddy's Car. 55
Bert's Lament 55
World Tour. 56
Fish out of Water. 58
Unkind Cuts 59
Danger Afoot 60
Just the Job. 62
Girl's Thoughts from a Train 65
Ready Wreckoner 66
That Painting: At Last the Truth 67
Thoughts 68
The Pheasant Shoot 68
The Rhinopotphantebeest. 69

The COMPLETE WIT & WHIMSEY

Advice to Travellers Abroad. 71
Theme and Variations.. 72
Fame at Last 73
Sort of a Bird 74
Song of the Happy Slug. 75
My Valentine 76
Snow White and the Seven Lonely Dwarves 76
Revision. 78
The Final Curtain. 79
Pedro the Pussy-Cat.. 80
Nursery Rhymes etc (revised). 81
A Family Sonnet 82
A Sugar-Free Sonnet. 83
Ode to the House-Dust Mite 83
The Earwig Supporters' Club. 84
Why People Write Poetry 84
The Sneeze. 84
Poem for Stephanie. 85
An Encounter with a Dish of *Mange-Tout* 86
All Screwed Up 87
WI, Oh, WI 88
My Satnav 90
Decade of Delight 91
Initial Reaction. 92
Finessing the Queen 94
Mother Knows Best. 97
Hero of our Time 99
Home Brew 100
Vocation. 101
Revenge of the Mice 102
Wedding Day Prayers 103

... and a few Bridge items ...
Making One Heart Non-Vulnerable 105
The Bridge Party 106
A Bridge Limerick. 107
My Bridge Valentine. 107
Cards on the Table 108

CONTENTS

Part 3 Limericks, non-Limericks, Clerihews and the Classics Revisited
Here you'll find 129 bits and pieces in a feast of original Limericks and similar verses 109

Part 4 In More Serious Vein
Grandpas. 119
A Military Education. 122
First Glimpse of War 124
Air Raid Scholars 126
Shift Workers. 127
Girls I Remember 128
There Was a Time 130
Ordeal 131
Summer Storm: Maryland 132
The Beach 134
Generations 135
Home 137
The Back Fields. 138
Hailes Abbey 139
The Deaf Shall Hear 141
Why 142
Aspects of Advent 143
Peace 144

and finally, Garden Sonnets
The Slug 145
The Worm 145
The Ant 145

The Woodlouse 145
The Honey Bee 146
The Centipede 146

The Spider 146
The Ladybird 146
The Butterfly 147

Index to first lines 148

The COMPLETE WIT & WHIMSEY

Part 1: STORIES & BALLADS

PART 1: A Few Stories and Ballads

This first poem takes us back to the beginning. I mean the absolute beginning when there was only one person around, called God, and nothing else existed until He decided to make a few things, like galaxies and people. But – were we the first?

RE CREATION

Thirty billion years ago
(Give or take a week or so),
God sat glumly on his own,
Contemplating life alone.
Feeling perhaps a touch annoyed,
He glared morosely at the void
And thought "That's it, then - no more waiting:
I'll spend the next six days creating.
*
He started work on one small planet
Made some limestone, made some granite,
Then, in wellies, spent some time
Laying down primordial slime.
The Big Bang came upon Day Four
With stars and galaxies galore
And, as he placed them in the sky
He thought "It's fun, this D.I.Y."
*
He sorted out the day from night:
How long the dark, how long the light.
He separated land from sea
(And thus invented Geography),
Then filled the planet overall
With plants and creatures great and small
Including one He called a horse
(Because it looked like one, of course.)
*
He made a man to look like Him,
Then made a woman from a limb.
Oh, sorry, no, I tell a fib:

He made her from the fellow's rib.
And, just to give them something nice
He made a place called Paradise.
"These things are good!" the Lord God thinks,
"And now it's time for forty winks."
*
But, sad to say, before too long
Upon the planet things went wrong:
'Twas Man that caused the dreadful mess
With politicians, tabloid press,
Famine, war and revolution,
Global warming, mass pollution,
Till at last all life was spent,
And then the full-time whistle went.
*
So, fifteen billion years ago
(Give or take a week or so)
God sat glumly on his own,
Contemplating life alone.
"Oh, well" he sighed, "I tried my best,
But Mankind simply failed the test.
I even sent my lad along
To teach the blighters right from wrong.
*
He put his feet up for a while,
But then he gave a thoughtful smile.
"Perhaps I didn't get it right.
I'll try again tomorrow night.
*
This time I'll make a place of worth
And call it - let me see now –
Earth."

The COMPLETE WIT & WHIMSEY

Let's stay with the religious theme: if you pick up your Bible, you won't have very far to look before you find the most famous of all love stories. Yes, it's right there in Genesis, Chapter 3. And here now is that wonderful story – in verse, of course.

ADAM'S APPLE

I

Another day in Paradise:
Adam stretched and rubbed his eyes
And studied Eve on bed of hay,
As naked on her back she lay.
Thought Adam, with a puckered brow,
'He's different, but I can't think how.'
Eve stirred, and climbed up from the hay
And said "Another gorgeous day!
I think I'll have a wander round,
There's bits of Eden I've not found.
I'll bring some food back for our lunch -
Some tasty fruit that we can munch."
"Then stay away from you-know-where,
I think I'd rather have a pear"
Said Adam, thinking back with dread
To words Almighty God had said.
"Don't worry, Adam, I'll watch out.
There's loads of other fruit about:
There's fig, banana, orange, banyan,
Damson, too" said his companion.
With that she ran off with a giggle,
Giving her behind a wiggle,
But this caused Adam not to fret
For sex was not invented yet.

II

Thought Adam 'What shall I do now?
Make a basket? Milk a cow?
Or perhaps I'll have a swim, and then
I'll practice counting one to ten.'
In fact, he whiled away the hours
By climbing trees, and picking flowers
Until at last Eve reappeared,
With an apple, as he'd feared.

III

She said "I met this sort of snake.
He pointed out which fruit to take."
But Adam screamed "You've brought a flippin'
Outlawed Cox's Orange Pippin!"
"Come on" she said, "Just have a taste,
We mustn't let it go to waste."
With that, she cut the fruit in two,
"There's half for me and half for you."
"OK" sighed Adam, "Let's not quibble"
And took a most reluctant nibble.
But then to his intense surprise
He felt the scales fall from his eyes.
"Why, you're a girl!" he cried with glee.
"And you're a man" said Eve, "Whoopee!
So now we've sorted out the muddle
Let's go and have a little cuddle."

IV

And so they did, but straight away
Eve put an end to fun and play
With those immortal words outrageous
Said by women down the ages:
"It's not that I don't like you - but
I think your toenails need a cut."
And handing him her apple parer
Said "Go on then, make them squarer."
So, with a sigh and looking pale
He shortened each offending nail.

Part 1: STORIES & BALLADS

V

That evening, as he took a walk,
Adam heard the Lord God talk:
"Where are you, Adam?" said the Voice.
'I'd better hide, I've little choice'
Thought Adam, crouching 'neath a bush
And gazing at the land of Cush.
"Why are you hiding?" said the Lord.
"Because I'm naked." "What!" He roared,
"How know you this? Ah, now I see,
You scrumped an apple from that tree.
For this you'll be forever banished."
"Please ...." Adam said. But God had vanished.

VI

"You're sure that's what he said?" asked Eve,
"That bit about we've got to leave?"
"Too right. I think we've got till Friday,
So let's at least leave Eden tidy."
Then with this task they 'gan to grapple:
Between the segments of the apple
Adam stuck each toenail bit -
A handy place, they seemed to fit.
Then, conscious of their sin horrendous,
In noting differences in genders,
They fastened fig-leaves, neat and trim,
Three for her and one for him;
And then they both picked up their goods
And set off glumly through the woods
Until they reached the edge of Eden.
"Come on" said Adam, "No use pleading."

VII

So Adam, followed by his mate,
Left Paradise and shut the gate.
And, thanks to their forbidden feast,
They wandered round the Middle East.
And from that day small toenail clippings
Are found in Cox's Orange Pippins.
In fact, all apples have a few.
I know I've seen them - haven't you?

Here is another Bible story in verse.

RAIN STOPPED PLAY

I

After God created Man
In strict accordance with his plan,
All went well for quite a while
Then, slowly, came a change of style:
As sin became regarded highly,
Mankind lived the life of Reilly,
Until at last God cried "Enough!
I'll put an end to all this stuff.
A flood will cover field and town
And everyone on Earth shall drown,
 - No, not quite all, I think I'll save a
Few in whom I find some favour.
I'll try to find me such a batch,
Then I can start again from scratch.
Now then, let's see, who's been most
  virtuous?
Yes, Noah's family's kind and courteous!"

II

Now Noah, I should really mention,
Had long been drawing old-age pension:
Six hundred years he'd been around,
Catching fish and tilling ground.
He had a wife and children three,
Strong lads were they, his progeny,
All born a hundred years before
(But folks lived long in days of yore).
Their names were Japheth, Ham and
  Shem
And all had wives - each one a gem.
So to this lovely, gentle bloke
Named Noah, God Almighty spoke:
"Hey Noah, Noah, 'tis the Lord."
And Noah, trembling, though "Oh,
  Gawd!"
The Lord said "Noah, though you're old
And frightened, just do what you're told.
Mankind is living so corruptly
I'm going to cancel them abruptly:
I'll make it rain. I've got my sights
On forty days and forty nights.
I'll drown the dumbest and the cleverest,
The flood will even cover Everest.
Believe me, these aren't idle menaces -
I'm getting sick and tired of Genesis.
Just one good family will I save
From going to a watery grave.
You, Noah, shall be my anointed,
In other words you've been appointed
Special servant here on Earth
To make Mankind a thing of worth."

III

Poor Noah was quite overcome
And felt his arms and legs go numb:
"Tell me, Lord, what I must do?
I'll surely need some help from you."
The Lord said "Go and build a boat,
 - An ark, the largest craft afloat.
Use gopher-wood for utmost strength,
Three hundred cubits make its length,
A width of fifty would be right,
And thirty cubits make its height.
Three decks construct, and then a roof,
And don't forget to waterproof.
My plan must work without a hitch,
So find out where to get some pitch.
Then go and look for every beast,
From huge ones to the very least,
And fish and fowl, and insects, too,
Of every shape and every hue,
And every creeping, crawling thing,
Both those that bite and those that sting.

Part 1: STORIES & BALLADS

Find every creature small and great,
One male, one female. Then they'll mate
When water levels have subsided
And to dry land your ark you've guided.
Now don't forget they'll need to feed,
So gather lots of hay and seed
And nuts to chew, and fruit to suck,
So get to work - and best of luck!"

IV

So Noah set to with a will,
With hammer, saw, and plane and drill.
His wife, his sons and their wives, too,
Joined in the task and saw it through.
And in the twenty-seventh week
They launched their ark upon a creek,
While other folks looked on in awe
And marvelled at the boat they saw,
But smiled when they heard Noah say
"It's something for a rainy day."
Said one chap, laughing, close to tears
"It hasn't rained for thirty years."
The crowd moved on, with winks and grins
To think up lots of nice new sins.

V

When the ark stood proud and tall,
Noah heard the Lord God call:
"I'm very pleased with you, my son.
This first task has been nicely done.
So now, dear children, I must ask
You all to do the other task
Before the rain comes pelting down
And sinful Man begins to drown."
"So when's this flood supposed to come?"
Asked Noah, looking rather glum.
"In seven days without a doubt"
Said God "So get your finger out.
Scour forest, mountain, lake and mead
To find the animals you need."

VI

The next few days passed in a whirl
As beastly boy and beastly girl
Were found and slowly settled in.
What a racket! What a din!
Roaring, chirping, squealing, bleating,
Till Noah called an urgent meeting.
He said "You hear that dreadful noise?
They want to play at girls and boys.
That's one thing we've all been forgetting:
If they spend half their time begetting
While we are drifting on the sea
There won't be room for you and me.
So sexes we must segregate.
That way they'll have no chance to mate."

VII

Just six days on, the boat was full
With sow and boar and cow and bull
And donkeys, horses, sheep and goats,
Rabbits, weasels, ferrets, stoats,
And thirty different breeds of frog
And fifty different breeds of dog:
Chihuahua, Border Collie, Beagle;
Birds galore from wren to eagle:
Birds of sea-shore, birds arboreal,
Swallow, swift and golden oriole,
Geese and swans and ducks and wigeons,
Cuckoos, starlings, doves and pigeons,
Herons, spoonbills, cranes and storks,
Buzzards, kestrels, sparrow-hawks,
And twenty different types of owl
And unpretentious farmyard fowl.
Tigers came, then bears and gnus
And wallabies and kangaroos.

VIII

The animals, both he and she 'un,
African, antipodean,
Were reasonably well-behaved,
Commands were given and obeyed
(Though one large lion in the bunch
Decided he'd have Ham for lunch,
Until a whack upon the hind
Persuaded him to change his mind.)
Monkeys, apes and chimpanzees
Obligingly supplied the fleas,
While several different breeds of lice
Were brought aboard by rats and mice.
The final animals were elks,
Then Shem arrived with crabs and whelks,
And Ham brought bowls containing plaice
And trout and salmon, roach and dace,
While Japheth bore a pair of boa
And other snakes to Father Noah.

VIII

Finally, the boat was ready,
Laden down, but holding steady.
They'd packed the final tit and lark
Into the creaking, squeaking ark,
The final finch, the final chiffchaff,
Then not surprisingly, the riff-raff
Started mocking them again:
"Nice boat" they said "But where's the rain?"
"We've every confidence in God"
Said Noah, "Soon the lands of Nod
And Eden will be flooded deep,
So now let's get a good night's sleep."
But as he spoke, he saw no cloud,
So, doubtfully, with shoulders bowed,
And with a slow shake of the head
He went to his reluctant bed.

IX

It started raining in the night,
Yes - God had got the forecast right
('Twas in the days ere Michael Fish
And Suzanne Charlton - what a dish!
And that impenetrable rascal
Ian what's-his-name McCaskill.)

X

'Neath sultry skies the air was warm.
Next day the rain became a storm,
The wind arose and blew a gale.
With lightening flashing came the hail.
The ark, behaving as bewitched,
Above the roiling water pitched,
While all around them, as they feared,
Towns and cities disappeared
And on the ocean strange things floated,
All disfigured, mostly bloated.
But God his hand he would not stay:
The waters, by the fifteenth day,
Had covered hills in Asia Minor
Deep enough to float a liner.

XI

Meanwhile, life upon the ark
Was pretty dreary, pretty stark,
As Noah and his wife and sons
Patrolled the cages and the runs,
Doling out the daily ration
Proper to each eating fashion.
Now lions, tigers and piranhas
Don't eat grapefruit or bananas,
So God told all the carnivora
"Leave the fauna, eat the flora."
But all this food engendered waste
To be disposed of with great haste,
- Not an easy operation
Without the beasts' cooperation.
So every night and every day
For guidance Noah used to pray:
He said "Lord, this is quite absurd,

Part 1: STORIES & BALLADS

We're ankle-deep in hippo turd,
And as for those confounded rhino,
Good job there's no such thing as lino.
We've also got a leopard crisis:
They've both come down with hepatitis."
"Don't worry, Noah," said the Lord,
"I know it's pretty grim on board,
But don't forget, the rain will stop
When waters reach the mountain top.
So don't despair, we're nearly there,
And soon the weather will be fair."

XII

It ceased to rain, but all was grey:
The dark cloud would not move away,
And thanks to global tidal motion
Over polar cap and ocean
The water rose before their gaze
For yet another hundred days.
Then one day, as they went on deck
To do the daily weather check
"I think the water's getting lower"
Optimistically said Noah,
"I wonder if there's land around."
The ark then gently went aground.
"Where are we, Noah?" called his wife,
"I couldn't guess to save my life."
And Noah said "It's rather murky,
But I'd say this was northeast Turkey."

XIII

The days went by, the flood receded,
So Noah knew his prayers were heeded.
He made a raven fly above
To scout for land, then sent a dove.
But both their recces were in vain
And so he sent the dove again
(He'd waited for a further week):
The dove returned with twig in beak.
He let another week go by
Then caused the dove again to fly,
Hoping even more to learn
Upon the little bird's return.

But no, the dove returned no more.
Said Noah "Time to go ashore."
But first of all, without a falter,
Noah built a simple altar,
And, showing not the least ambivalence,
Thanked the Lord for their deliverance.
"And look at this!" he gave a shout,
"At last the sun is coming out!"

XIV

The creatures formed an eager queue
To leap ashore and start to woo.
Said Mrs Noah "It's a blow
To let these friendly creatures go.
For every day I just got fonder
Even of the anaconda."
Said Noah "I agree, my dear,
But goodness me, what have we here?
We kept the sexes well apart
(And that itself was quite an art),
But animals have inter-bred:
New species have been born instead.
Now I remember, yes, of course,
I put the donkey with the horse!"

XV

Once again the Lord God spoke
To Noah and the other folk.
He said "Before your very eyes
I'm going to spring a great surprise."
And, as the dark clouds moved away,
They saw a bow in colours gay.
Said God "This rainbow is a sign
That Man is now a friend of mine.
Whatever sins he perpetrates
We're going to be the best of mates.
Henceforth I'll spare Man and his
    creatures
And never mar again Earth's features."
So Noah and his kin on board
Thanked God for such a grand reward.

XVI

And since that time the rainbow sign
Has painted skies 'mid rain and shine,
- A brilliant, everlasting token
That God has not his promise broken.
And, though it might seem otherwise,
'Neath British Spring and Summer skies,
We know He will not press again
His lever marked "Excessive Rain."

And before we leave the Bible and all things spiritual.......

GOD LOVES ATHEISTS. TOO

I'd like to go to Heaven,
I'd like to earn my place
So I can be there just to witness
Richard Dawkins' face.

Part 1: STORIES & BALLADS

I'm sure we've all met snobs – people who look down their noses at others. They tend to mix with their own kind, and stay away from "common" people. But occasionally paths do cross. And what happens then? Well, let's find out. This is what happened when one particularly snooty lady encountered a gentleman from the other side of town.

A BIT OF ROUGH

Mrs Spencer-Smythe looks down
On those the other side of town.
She's lived alone since Henry died,
A widow, poised and dignified.

Mrs Spencer-Smythe belittles
Those involved with beer and skittles.
She invariably snubs
Anyone who visits pubs.

Mrs Spencer-Smythe disdains
Those who show a lack of brains.
(She herself has boundless knowledge
Gained within a Ladies' College.)

Mrs Spencer-Smythe condemns
Skirts with elevated hems.
Skirts should always, if you please,
Come some way below the knees

And she will frequently disparage
Unions thriving outside marriage.
She was wed for forty years
Till Henry's death turned joy to tears.

But now we see her in her room,
Reminiscing in the gloom.
She muses for a little while
And then permits herself a smile.

It happened when she came from church:
She saw this man towards her lurch.
He'd had a few pints in a pub,
Now made his way towards the Club,

An oldish fellow, not a youth,
Ill-mannered, tipsy and uncouth.
She'd seen him shopping here and there –
A widower with curly hair.

His home was in a run-down flat.
It seemed that he admired her hat.
He'd shouted "Missus, you look great.
I'd love to have a tête à tête.

So come and see me when you're free,
I lives at number twenty-three.
We'll have some bread and cheese and pickle,
Then a bit of slap and tickle!"

He'd worn a sort of sleeveless vest
And hair stuck up around his chest.
Tattoos adorned his muscled arms -
And yet, she'd not the slightest qualms.

For, as he'd left with loud guffaws,
He'd caused her ladyship to pause.
She'd not cried out her opposition,
But quietly weighed his proposition.

Since Henry's death she'd craved a friend
To be there till the bitter end.
She felt quite fit, and stayed quite active,
And *someone* thought her still attractive.

She also needed, as a friend,
A man whose ways she could amend.
She'd managed it as Henry's wife,
Improving him throughout his life.

She wouldn't like that dreadful flat:
He'd move in here, and that was that.
Together, they would live in sin!
She smiled - and poured another gin.

The COMPLETE WIT & WHIMSEY

No matter how healthy you've been all your life, as soon as you get to middle-age things start going wrong – especially things above the neck: your ears and eyes don't work so well or your teeth start dropping out. Well, here's the story of someone this happened to – one of the healthiest people you could imagine – a wonderful old Welsh shepherd called Dewi Morgan, who lived in one of those villages the Welsh seem able to spell without the benefit of a vowel! This poem is called "The Bottom Line."

THE BOTTOM LINE

Dewi Morgan earned his keep
By tending herds of mountain sheep.
He spent all day up on the hill
And never felt the least bit ill.
But then, when he reached sixty-three
His teeth hurt when he drank his tea,
And at the age of sixty-four
He found them hurting even more,
So knew he'd have to make a date
To have some out, and get a plate.

*

His drinking pals gave their advice:
Checking teeth may not suffice.
You need to check out all your head"
Said Pete the Meat and Fred the Bread.
When you reach sixty, most things go -
It isn't just your teeth, you know.
The very least that you should do
Is get your eyesight tested, too."

*

So Dewi Morgan, with a frown,
Caught the bus that went to town
And when he got there paid a call
Upon the dentist known to all
As Keith the Teeth, who said "Oh, dear
I think we've got some trouble here.
I'm going to have to pull a few,
But soon your mouth will look like new.
You won't have very long to wait:
In four weeks time you'll have your plate.

You'll soon feel proud to smile and speak,
I'll take your teeth out Monday week,
But now just bite into this stuff.
And for today that's quite enough."
So Dewi, on that opening session
Made a very good impression.

*

Then, as he left to go, he said
"I need to check out all my head.
My pals advised an eyesight test.
If you can't do it, who's the best?
Said Keith "The man you need is Dai.
He's known round here as Dai the Eye.
So why not fix it for the date
You come back to collect your plate?"

*

In four weeks time, without a fuss,
Came Dewi Morgan on the bus.
He got his teeth and put them in
And slowly tried a practice grin:
Oh, what a vision! What a sight!
He smiled and smiled in sheer delight.
He laughed and giggled, slapped his thigh,
Then off he went to Dai the Eye.

Part 1: STORIES & BALLADS

And Dai said "Dewi, see that chart?
Well, read it to me from the start."
So Dewi started at the top
And carried on without a stop.
"Well done" said Dai, "You're doing fine.
Now what about the bottom line.
Try to read it to me please.
Can you read that line with ease?"

So Dewi gave the line a scan.
"Ha! Can I read it? Course I can"
He flashed a smile with brand-new teeth,
"I've been there, man, it's just near
　Neath!"

The COMPLETE WIT & WHIMSEY

As a writer, naturally I love words and especially the subtle difference between words with similar meanings. Not surprisingly, one of the books I consult most often is good old Roget's Thesaurus. Now I've often wondered what it might be like working for such a publication. And what might happen if two employees, two lexicographers there, actually fell in love with each other. Well, here's a poem to illustrate what might just happen in that situation. It's called "It's Love (In So Many Words)".

IT'S LOVE (in so many words)

In the claustrophobic gloom
Of a musty, fusty room,
Works a silent band of souls
Pursuing literary goals.
Some are women, some are men,
Cloistered in a common den.
No sound must pass from any lip
To interrupt their scholarship
And thus the master plan negate:
To bring Thesaurus up to date.

A young man raises eye from books,
And warily around him looks.
He trembles as he catches sight
(Some twenty metres to the right)
Of a slender, dark-eyed lass,
Who must think he's a perfect ass,
For every time he steals a glance
She's looking at him, all askance.
This situation has been so
Since Monday, fifteen weeks ago
(A day of rather nasty weather),
When both had joined the staff together.
Now, after all this time spent near her,
She every day to him grows dearer.
He dare not speak to her with candour
And only knows her name: Amanda
(A feminine gerundive, Latin).
He gazes at the chair she's sat in:
'You're beautiful' he softly sighs,
Then blushes and averts his eyes.

At last he summons up the nerve
His amorous intent to serve.
He overhears her in the lift
(At least he thinks he's caught the drift):
It seems her birthday's next weekend.
Perhaps a little note he'll send
To ask her if she wouldn't care
The theatre and a meal to share.
His birthday's only nine days later,
So what a splendid time to date her
(He's Gemini and she is Taurus).
His research for the New Thesaurus
Silently he thrusts aside
And deftly manages to hide
The note he pens to dear Amanda
Which, clandestinely, he will hand her.

Now, from his corner ventures he,
On call of nature, doubtlessly.
He smiles, and as he passes by her,
Pulse *allegro,* cheeks on fire,
Drops the little note, and thence
He sidles off to seek the Gents.

Amanda can't believe her eyes
And views the missive with surprise,
Then, making sure that no-one heeds,
His words with interest she reads:
"My dear Amanda" (said the note)
"I felt it high time that I wrote

Part 1: STORIES & BALLADS

(Or copied, penned, or did some scrawl)
To let you know that, above all,
It's you I love *(admire, revere,*
Adore and dote on). So, my dear
(Or honey, darling, jewel, moppet,
Idol, sweetheart, baby, poppet),
Would you care to have a meal?
This Saturday would be ideal
(Or optimum, select, or choice,
See four-eight-oh for verdict, voice),
And then a visit to a play
(Stage production, matinée?)
Please tell me that you will say 'yes'
(Concur, assent or acquiesce).
Affectionately I remain,
Your true admirer *(suitor, swain,*
Your paramour, adorer, beau,
Your follower and lover) - Joe."

What could she do? She loved him, too,
So typed a little billet doux
And left it on his desk at one,
When he had popped out for a bun.
Then later, when he read the note,
Joe felt a lump come in his throat.
Amanda's note said "Dearest Joe
Your letter gave me such a glow
(Or tingle, tremor, blush, suffusion,
Thrill, excitement, shock, confusion).
I'd love to spend some time with you
And be together, just the two
(Or deuce, or couple, brace or pair).
How do you fancy Leicester Square?
I think that's where we ought to meet,
Then find a little place to eat
(Or swallow, gobble, nibble, munch,
Gorge, devour, or gulp or crunch)
And then perhaps a little walk:
In theatres it's hard to talk
(Recite, declaim, address or preach,
Soliloquize or make a speech).
I'll close now, with best wishes and a
Little kiss from yours, Amanda.

And so began the big romance:
He took her out to dine and dance
And (mingling with the sporting hordes)
Twickenham, the Oval, Lords.
Their wedding was a great success.
Amanda, what a lovely dress!
And all the staff from New Thesaurus
Sang her favourite hymn in chorus
(With the church choir, standing dutiful):
The one called "All Things Bright and
 Beautiful
(Or seemly, bonny, graceful, slick,
Sightly, dashing, stylish, chic,
Lovely, handsome, pretty, fair,
Neat, resplendent, debonair)."

The COMPLETE WIT & WHIMSEY

Many years ago a form of verse known as the barrack-room ballad was born. I'm not sure if Rudyard Kipling actually invented them, but he certainly popularised them in the late 19th and early 20th centuries. These ballads usually told of strange events in Army life. Well, here's a modern barrack-room ballad. It tells the tale of a simple soldier who became the victim of a clerical error and suddenly found he was a senior officer assigned to the Ministry of Defence – or M.O.D. as it's known – a Government Department which occupies a resplendent building off Whitehall, with beautiful female figures flanking the imposing entrance. This barrack-room ballad is entitled "Sins of Commission."

SINS OF COMMISSION (a modern barrack-room ballad)

Oh, they talks of it in Naafi's
And in pubs and even cafes,
And wherever soldiers sips their beer and tea:
'Ow a Corporal of the Tanks
Got promoted from the ranks
'Cos his record 'ad an 'o' and not a 'p'.

*

Some thought it was a lark
When the little postings clerk
Transferred Corporal Kelly up to M.O.D.
Then it seemed a 'uge mistake
(Like the Army's prone to make)
When 'is record 'ad an 'o' and not a 'p'.

*

Now your Corporal's C-p-l
And your Colonel's C-o-l.
When you're typin', 'p' and 'o's adjacent, see,
And in Corporal Kelly's record
(Where it said red-'eaded, freckled),
Well, they went and put an 'o' instead of 'p'.

*

Now I know it sounds quite barmy,
But throughout the British Army
What your record says is what you gotter be,
And an error most infernal
Changed a Corporal to a Colonel
'Cos they went and put an 'o' instead of 'p'.

*

There 'ad been a Colonel Kelly
(And 'e'd even been on telly),
Like the Corporal, 'is initial was a 'T'.
But on leave 'e went a-sailin'
And was leanin' on the railin'
When 'e fell and then got drownded out at sea.

*

When the records got updated,
Corporal Kelly, quite elated,
Found 'isself transferred as 'Kelly, Colonel T',
But 'e wasn't gonna quarrel
'Cos that woulda been immoral
But 'e guessed they'd put an 'o' instead of 'p'.

*

So 'e goes to M.O.D.
Where the naked ladies be,
Wot stands guard above the steps as you goes in,
And on the second floor
Found an office with a door
Wot said 'Colonel Kelly T' and made 'im grin.

Part 1: STORIES & BALLADS

And 'e 'ad a staff of twenty:
Captains, Majors there was plenty,
And 'arf-Colonels, well they reckons there was three,
And 'is job says 'Future Plans' -
Workin' out where NATO stands
On things like armour and artillery.

*

Well, 'e gets some Board Report
And 'e read it and 'e thought
I don't know a lot, but 'ell, I knows me tanks.
And this tank they're gonna buy
(Without a word of lie)
Was designed by people thick as two short planks.

*

So 'e whispers in the ear
Of 'is boss, the Brigadier,
'Oo says "Really. What do you know about tanks?"
So Kelly, full of smiles,
Says "I 'elped to do the trials:
A lot of work and very little thanks.

*

Oh, this tank goes very fast
But it's not designed to last:
It's an engineerin' nightmare to maintain.
If it breaks down in a fight
You can kiss the crew goodnight
'Cos you'll never start the bloody thing again.

*

There was blokes from lots of nations
Doin' these evaluations,
I can see 'em now, all lined up in a row,
And accordin' to the Yanks
They preferred the British tanks
And was goin' to let their Army Generals know.

*

By the time the trials was ended,
Well, the 'ole team recommended
That we shouldn't buy this tank for NATO use.
Our advice 'as been ignored
By the people on this Board.
Well, I 'opes they got a bloody good excuse!"

*

So the Brigadier says "Well,
You're an expert, I can tell -
The first we've ever 'ad in M.O.D.
If you find some lack of vision
It's because the Board's decision
Is political, not military, you see."

*

Well, young Kelly goes beserk
And 'e really sets to work
Phonin' everyone wot took part in the trials.
And their Generals sent their thanks
And confirmed they wanted tanks
Wot was manufactured in the British Isles.

*

Well we knows wot 'appened then:
There was calls to Number Ten
From the 'eads of all these countries far and near.
So the Board with great delight
Quickly put the matter right
And Kelly? 'E was made a Brigadier.

*

That's the story as it's told
Among soldiers young and old,
But there's quite a bit that no-one will reveal,
And near Whitehall's busy hub
In a fashionable club
Two gentlemen will sometimes share a meal.

They still recall the drama
Over NATO's choice of armour,
And continue their discussion in the bar,
Where the Most Distinguished Soldier
Says "We fixed it, as I told you.
Wasn't easy, but then these things
    seldom are.
          *

What we needed was precision
To reverse a bad decision,
And a terrier who wouldn't leave things be,
And we knew that Corporal Kelly
Had this brimstone in his belly
And he also knew his subject to a T.
          *

But, though expert on the tank,
He just didn't have the rank
To do a proper job in M.O.D.
So I scanned the Army journals
For obituaries of Colonels
And just happened to alight on Kelly T.
          *

So the records then got merged
And a little bit got purged
But things like that, of course, we never
    mention.
They're often much maligned,
But computers now, I find,
Are becoming a significant invention!"
          *

Says the other "Give our thanks
To your Corporal from the Tanks,
And I'm glad you've made the chap a
    Brigadier."
(He was one of those civilians
Whose face was known to millions),
"But is that really best for his career?"
          *

The Soldier says "Why, yes,
We can't undo this mess,
So a Brigadier the blighter's got to stay.
With his belly full of fire
He could even go on higher -
And he'd never get to Sergeant, anyway!"

Part 1: STORIES & BALLADS

Rupert Brooke and W H Auden, among others, would often lace their poetry with bits of another language, notably Greek or German, yet retain the rhyme. It's an interesting challenge this, including foreign words, yet preserving rhyme and metre, as in this little story. On the other hand, perhaps this makes things easier – more choice!

A BREAKFAST SERIAL (IN TWENTY SERVINGS)

I

Some years ago, I understand,
In the Bernese Oberland
There lived a poor but honest farmer
With his Frau, *ein grosse Dame.*
She towered above him by a metre,
She was Anna, he was Dieter.
They had a son whose name was Hans,
He was quite small, *ja, klein er, ganz,*
And a buxom daughter, Gretchen,
Considered *ein sehr schönes Mädchen.*
Theirs was a miserable existence,
Eking out a bare subsistence
With seven cows and fifteen hens,
A pig or two, enclosed in pens.
They also had a friendly mule
Upon their holding miniscule.
They didn't own the land, you see.
For theirs was just a tenancy.
They paid their rent to Rheinhard Stern,
Who journeyed up each month from Berne,
A landlord quite devoid of malice.
But Dieter's problem, *über alles,*
Was finding every month the rent
Because he earned less than he spent.
Whenever Rheinhard would appear
They'd feed him well and give him beer,
And Gretchen would bestow a kiss,
A bit of that, a bit of this.
They hoped thereby they could delay
The day when Rheinhard made them pay.

II

One day, the next for monthly reckoning,
Dieter saw his Anna beckoning.
"There's nothing much to eat" she said,
"We have *kein* bacon, ham or bread.
I've only got dried fruit and flour,
And Rheinhard comes in just one hour.
I quite forgot this was his day,
So how are we to feed him, pray?"
"Now, don't despair" said husband Dieter,
"Have you got milk?" "*Ja,* several litre."
"Then I know just what you can make:
Those little scones you used to bake.
That was how you won my heart.
So hurry, *Liebchen,* make a start."
"I'll need some help" his wife declared,
And Dieter simply stood and stared.
"But we are busy, too, dear Frau,
Hans must feed the mule right now
And I must saw the winter logs
Then milk the cows and feed the hogs."
"Well, where is Gretchen? *Was tut sie?*"
"She's feeding chickens, dear" said he.
"Then come as quickly as you can!"
She turned away and grabbed a pan.

III

The mule was Hans's pride and joy
He'd fed it since he was a boy.
The food he used came by the can,
Two special types of Scottish bran:
A summer and a winter mix
With stuff to keep away the ticks
And extra protein in the feed

That came from nuts and sunflower seed.
On every can one could behold
Stencilled on in letters bold
"James McGregor, Aberdeen
By appointment to the Queen
Purveyors of all livestock feed."
And underneath this, one could read
In letters very tall and wide
The contents to be found inside:
(Complying with the export rules)
"Horses", "Ponies", "Donkeys", "Mules".
The final message of the printer
Was "1" for summer, "2" for winter.
The present can of "Mules" feed "1"
Was almost empty, nearly done,
And just as Hans took off the lid
(The first thing that he always did),
He heard his father loudly call
"Your Mother's going up the wall.
She needs some help from me and you.
I'd better find your sister, too!"
So Hans went off to do his duty
To help his rather fearsome *Mutti,*
Still clutching can of "Mules" feed "1",
A very kind, obedient son.

IV

Meanwhile, at the chicken coops,
Gretchen doled out healthy scoops
Of corn, and bits of oyster shard
That made the eggshells nice and hard,
Singing in contralto cheery
Melodies of the Valkyrie,
And when those extracts had been sung,
She turned to *Gottedämmerung.*
'Twas then she heard her father shout
"Go and help your Mother out.
Rheinhard's due in half an hour
So hurry now, my little flower."
"Ah, lovely Rheinhard" sighed the girl,
Brushing back an errant curl.
"For Rheinhard nothing but the best,
But *Himmel* - just look how I'm dressed!"
And to the house she ran pell-mell
With pail of corn and oyster shell.

V

In the woodshed Dieter swore,
And finally threw down his saw.
"I'd better go and help my wife
If only for a peaceful life."
So, muttering Teutonic oaths,
With sawdust clinging to his clothes,
Gritting teeth and clenching fist,
He strode in silence to assist.

VI

Glancing at the cuckoo-clock,
Anna noted with a shock
That less than half an hour remained.
There'd be no scones and she'd be
    blamed.
Or else he wouldn't like the taste
Because she'd had to work in haste.
Then, as she seized a large blue jug,
Her feet tripped on the kitchen rug.
The milk poured down upon the floor
And quickly ran towards the door,
Covering the kitchen tiles
- A thin white lake with small red isles,
While Anna, trying not to fall,
Ricocheted against the wall
And thrashing out with all her power
Brought down her bowl of fruit and flour.

VII

Just then young Hans came in to help.
He lost his feet and gave a yelp.
The mule feed scattered everywhere
(Some even landed in his hair).

Part 1: STORIES & BALLADS

VIII

Across the tiles so wet and slick
Came Gretchen now with footsteps quick,
Described an arabesque of grace
And promptly landed on her face,
While chicken feed and oyster shell
In little heaps about her fell.

IX

Then, lastly through the door came Dieter
And very soon began to teeter.
He ended up upon his rear,
Dispensing sawdust far and near.

X

Poor Anna wailed in great distress
"Just look at all this bloody mess!
No food to eat and Rheinhard due.
Now what the hell we going to do?"
Said Dieter, feeling rather sore,
"At least there's time to sweep the floor.
And Gretchen must be extra nice,
I mean not once, but maybe twice,
And if we fill him full of beer
He may forget the rent, my dear."
Since no-one had a better plan
Hans found the empty mule-feed can.
"We'll put it all in here" he cried,
"The floor has very nearly dried."

XI

Minutes later, when they'd done,
In the can of "Mules" feed "1",
Were sawdust, flour, and bits of fruit,
And corn and oyster shell, to boot.
Nuts and sunflower seed and bran,
All were shovelled in the can
With other things that lay around:
Dead flies and spiders' legs they found
And culinary marginalia
From long-forgotten kitchen failure.

XII

No sooner had the mess been cleared
Than Rheinhard at the door appeared,
A large man, full of repartee,
An amiable giant, he.
But now he looked a little worn
After travelling since dawn.
"*Grüss Gott*", he grinned, "And how are you?
I hope you've made my favourite stew,
Or perhaps some eggs and home-cured ham,
And fresh-baked bread, and Anna's jam."
He pointed to his stomach cavernous,
"To tell the truth, I'm slightly ravenous."
He shook with laughter at his joke,
Then lit a pipe and had a smoke.
Said Anna, rather nervously,
"We'd planned this small surprise, you see.
"I love surprises" Rheinhard roared,
"But where's my Gretchen?" he implored.
"She's gone to change" her mother said,
"She's just come from the chicken shed.
But I'll make sure she knows you're here."
"And I'll go off and get some beer"
Said Dieter, "It's my special brew."
Poor Hans was not sure what to do,
Then "I must feed the mule" he blurted.
And Rheinhard found himself deserted.

XIII

While he sat there all alone,
Rheinhard's stomach gave a groan.
'They said they'd planned a small surprise'
He mused, and idly let his eyes
Survey the kitchen of the cottage,
Searching for a mess of pottage.
And, as he slowly made his scan,
His eyes alighted on a can
Standing near a jug of cream.
He looked inside, and gave a beam.

XIV

No-one was eager to return
To face a starving Rheinhard Stern,
Until some fifteen minutes later
Gretchen entered with her mater:
They saw the jug, they saw the can,
They saw the bowl, they saw the man,
They saw a spoon in rapid motion.
Then they heard a great commotion:
Through the far door, looking pale,
Barged Dieter with a cask of ale,
About to interrupt the meal
That Rheinhard tackled with great zeal.
But then he stopped instead to stare,
To halt the meal he did not dare,
Sensing the outlandish food
Was acting as a force for good.

XV

Rheinhard's face was all aglow.
They heard him murmur soft and low
"How kind they are, such nuts, such fruit,
Such wholesome food - *es schmeckt sehr gut.*"
He ate as much as he was able
Then pushed the chair back from the table.
He sang a little song, *con brio*,
And glancing round, he saw the trio.
"My friends" he said, with tearful eyes,
"That was a wonderful surprise.
No rent you'll have to pay today,
And now I must be on my way."
Poor Gretchen, overcome with shock,
Resplendent in her only frock,
Said "Rheinhard, must you really go?
We haven't even said hello."
"Yes, yes" cried Rheinhard, "I must see
The owner of a factory.
That food I had is something which
Is marketable - you'll be rich.
Now, this is what you have to do:
Just mix another can or two
Exactly like today's edition,
Identical in composition.
And I'll be back in three days time.
It's worth the journey, worth the climb.
Two cans to start with will be ample.
We only need a modest sample
To ascertain the public's views,
And if it sells we'll mass-produce.
Now what's it called?" He then began
To copy what was on the can.
"These words I do not understand,
But still, we'll use it as the brand."
With that, he set off to return
By horseback and by rail to Berne.

XVI

The family grinned at one another,
Father, daughter and her mother.
They hugged and kissed and danced and sang
And cheered until the rafters rang;
Then drank a toast to Rheinhard's health
And possibilities of wealth.
But then, when things became less hectic:
"You know that Rheinhard is dyslectic,
He's bad enough in German-Swiss,
I don't know what he'll make of this"
Said Gretchen, pointing to the can
Of "Mules 1" special summer bran.
Said Dieter "Well, that may be true,
But come, we've lots of work to do.
I'll make some sawdust, quite enough,
You, Gretchen, get the chicken stuff.
Tell Hans to bring some summer mix,
Five basins full, or maybe six.
And Anna, fetch a sack of flour
And find some fruit. In half an hour
We'll meet back here, and then we'll pour
The whole lot on the kitchen floor,
Then sweep it up with brooms and pans
And tip it in two empty cans."

XVII

They fetched and carried, measured, sawed,
Each item on the floor they poured.
They went in search of spiders' legs
And flies, and sundry kitchen dregs.
At last their task they had achieved,
So drank some beer and felt relieved.

XVIII

Three days later, Rheinhard Stern
Travelled up from distant Berne,
Stayed not for victuals or libations
Or Gretchen's tender ministrations.
He wrapped the cans in large, clean rags
And stuffed them in his saddle-bags.
Then off he went, success to seek
And said he'd be back in a week.
So, Dieter's family, somewhat lost,
Waited with their fingers crossed.

XIX

A week went by then, full of joy.
Came Rheinhard, like a little boy.
"The public love it" he declared,
"Much more than even I had dared
To hope. And so we'll mass-produce.
I think you'll now have little use
For farming, for I need your skill
To run the process at the mill:
Honest people, strong and wise
To oversee our enterprise.
I've found some bankers who will back it."
He then produced a cardboard packet.
"Here's how we plan to market it,
With middle-classes targetted."
They gathered round to view the box,
Then Gretchen, shaking flaxen locks,
Gave out a sigh both loud and long
"I knew he'd get the writing wrong!"

XX

Five years passed by, gone were their cares,
For all of them were millionaires.
They now had staff to run the mill,
To mix things up and boxes fill.
And Gretchen, long now Rheinhard's wife,
Would ponder on her former life:
On how strange things had shaped events,
Like "Mules 1" feed and unpaid rents.
'Mid sawdust, nuts and spiders' legs,
Oyster shards for hard-shelled eggs,
Dyslexia, and bran and corn,
The Muesli empire had been born.

The COMPLETE WIT & WHIMSEY

There's a tiny bit of fantasy in this poem. It presents what for me would be a perfect outcome of Anglo-French civic cooperation.

THE FRENCH CONNECTION

I

In Picardy there stands a town
Of imperceptible renown:
Its name is Crépy (pop. two thou' -
You haven't heard of it till now?
Although perhaps you might declare
They probably make pancakes there?)
This lack of fame brought much concern
Aux habitants, les vieux, les jeunes.

II

And so, *Monsieur le Maire* et al.
(i.e. *Conseil Municipal*)
Declared they must reverse the trend:
Their anonymity must end.
Les habitants, both rich and poorest
Stood to gain much from the tourist
If they could inspiration tap
To put their borough on the map.

III

Then someone said "*Un Festival
Ou littéraire ou musical.*"
But no, the Mayor could not agree
To a,b,c or doh-ray-me
Because, he said, he never read,
Apart from *Figaro* in bed.
"What's more, I haven't" said the Mayor,
"Even got a record-player!"

IV

And so they had another think,
And someone offered wine to drink,
Considering a small libation
Always fosters inspiration.
And soon a girl said "*S'il vous plaît*,
Let's find a nice *ville jumelée* -
A twin town, eh, *Monsieur le Maire,
En Allemagne, en Angleterre?*"

V

The Mayor, to start with, was in doubt,
Not sure what this was all about,
But very soon gave his consent,
When told exactly what it meant:
That, though there were some silly rules,
Like student swaps between the schools,
Villes jumelées outside *La France*
Were where *les Maires* got free
    vacances.

VI

The Mayor said "Make it *Angleterre,*
There aren't so many Germans there.
I rather like the ferry, but'll
Gladly ride aboard *Le Shuttle.*
And now, it just remains our task
To choose the town we ought to ask.
Though power to us has been devolved,
Let's get *Les Citoyens* involved."

VII

And so a letter was composed
Explaining what the Mayor proposed,
With tear-off slip for writing down
Suggestions for the choice of town.
However, it was soon quite clear
That some had got the wrong idea,
Or else they'd falsely held from birth
That *Angleterre* bestrode the earth.

VIII

Ideas included Casablanca,
Kansas City and Sri Lanka,
Copenhagen, Alma Ata,
Minsk, Vancouver and Jakarta,
While those that chose an English town
Hadn't thought to scale it down
As London, Birmingham and Leeds
Were thought to fit the borough's needs.

Part 1: STORIES & BALLADS

IX
Some even thought Montpellier
A suitable *ville jumelée*,
While others gave advice on where
The people ought to send the Mayor:
And here they sang the self-same tune -
His journey's end, of course, *La Lune*.
At last the Mayor cried "That's enough,
I don't like this facetious stuff.
Let's seek advice from Monsieur Brown,
The only Englishman in town."

X
Now Monsieur Brown was much admired:
A former teacher, now retired
Who, some time in his student days
Had met his wife, *une belle française*.
He'd taught in England, taught in France,
And now, he quietly nurtured plants.

XI
He listened to the Mayor's request
And promised that he'd do his best.
Then, after thinking matters through
He knew exactly what to do:
The people here - they were his life,
They'd even given him a wife.
Their innocence had struck a chord.
Surely it deserved reward.

XII
So Nigel Brown, the francophile,
Sat him down and, with a smile,
A kindly, thoughtful letter penned
To a former college friend
Whose erudition waxed prolific
On anything the least bit civic.
And in the general Sussex region
His useful contact points were legion.

XIII
He emphasised this was no joke:
He really wished to help these folk.
And, sure enough, some six weeks after,
Nigel's 'phone shed peals of laughter
As a certain Sussex Mayor
Said "Yes, we'd make a lovely pair,
Your town and ours - it takes the prize,
Although we're forty times your size!

XIV
So tell your friends that we agree.
I'll write and tell them formally.
We'll even make a lovely sign
To show we're honoured to combine.
And then to Crépy we can go,
And do some sort of Mayoral show:
Make a speech, present the sign,
Stick it up and drink some wine.

XV
They'll flock from England just to see
The sign that shows our unity:
In fact, two local travel firms
Are even now deciding terms.
There's money in it, pounds and francs -
We'll all go laughing to the banks!"
The Sussex Mayor then bade 'Good-bye'
While Nigel breathed a happy sigh.

XVI
And that's precisely what took place:
The two towns opted to embrace,
Then French and English delegations
Joined each other's celebrations.
And tourists now stop off to dine
And giggle at the twin-town sign
Painted large in colours gay:
"Crépy-Crawley: Jumelées".

XVII
(I trust the reader won't resent it,
But this story, as presented,
Strays a little from the fact,
For those involved have yet to act.
But wouldn't it provide a stir
If these events were to occur?
It only takes one fearless Mayor
To act with skill, with style, with flair!)

The COMPLETE WIT & WHIMSEY

Whenever it's winter, I always remember the time when a man sitting on his JCB digging a trench on a building site cut through a cable, and as a result there was no power in our village from mid-day until the evening. And what chaos that created! No lighting, no heating, no cooking with electricity, no fridges or TV's working. Well, here's a little poem based on that crisis. It's called "When Charlie Cut the Cable".

WHEN CHARLIE CUT THE CABLE

When Charlie cut the cable
One freezing winter's day.
He caused a bit of havoc
And some said he ought to pay.
But everyone likes Charlie,
He's always full of cheer,
It's just that on his JCB
He's rather cavalier.
He really loves his holes, though,
They fill each waking hour,
And sitting up there in his cab
He's got this sense of power.

When Charlie cut the cable
'Twas very nearly noon
And lunch was getting underway
Inside the Silver Spoon.
But when the power went down they found
They couldn't boil or fry,
So ham and tuna salad
Took the place of Cottage Pie.
And, though they couldn't heat the soup,
They sold it by the bowl
And served it cold, with letters bold:
'Gazpacho Español'.

When Charlie cut the cable
Hair Today were cross
And Madame Yvonne (Karen Jones)
Bemoaned financial loss.
For, ever since the final rinse,
They hadn't any heat,

So three old girls with sopping curls
Ran wailing down the street.
They caught a chill and all fell ill,
Then Mrs. Brown got worse,
But folks were glad because she had
A really lovely hearse.

When Charlie cut the cable
The Co-op had to close,
As cabinets of perishables
 Gradually unfroze.
And the automatic check-outs -
Well, of course, they wouldn't run,
And nobody could manually
Dot and carry one.
Then all the shops just followed suit,
 First one, and then another,
Except for Reg in fruit and veg.
 - But then, he'd sell his Mother!

When Charlie cut the cable
The dentist stopped his drilling,
He was only half way through the job
So couldn't do the filling.
 And at the Cottage Hospital,
It made them stop and think:
'Cos their stand-by generator
Was also on the blink.
They had these fall-back measures
And considered their adoption,
But vasectomy by candlelight
Is not a happy option.

CONTENTS

When Charlie cut the cable
The power was off all day:
By half past three folks couldn't see,
So left work right away.
But back at home they had no heat,
No TV and no light,
And so instead they went to bed
Till someone put things right.
The Company were on the ball:
They sent a crew of three,
Who worked quite late - till nearly eight
With just six stops for tea.

When Charlie cut the cable
It paralysed the village,
But everyone was well-behaved -
There was no rape or pillage.
And, like I said, folks went to bed,
With nothing else to do,
But some remember that December
With a smile or two:
Fourteen babies come along
(Honest - cross my heart!)
And two looked just like Charlie - but
Lived seven miles apart!

The COMPLETE WIT & WHIMSEY

Remember the Starship Enterprise? Well, it finally got back to Earth, and what a welcome awaited the intrepid Captain and his brave crew. Let's look back at (or forward to) that momentous occasion.

TO BOLDLY RETURN

A million miles above the skies
Between the moon and sun,
Here comes the Starship Enterprise,
Its ten-year mission done.

The members of the crew all know
Their time was richly spent:
They'd said they'd planned "to boldly go",
And so they boldly went.

And now they're coming home again
Their welcome to enjoy.
And as they race towards the Earth
Their sensors they deploy.

"Just focus on the landing site",
The Captain said to Spock,
"They're sure to greet us with delight
And mob us when we dock."

Said Spock "You see that massive troupe?
I knew our screen would show it.
It's certainly a Welcome Group
But not, Jim, as we know it.

Those men in uniforms of black,
I can't think what their job is.
They're at the front and at the back
And look like London bobbies."

The spaceship glides beneath the cloud
They land their famous craft,
And right away the seething crowd
Press near them, fore and aft.

The automatic gangway drops,
The crew emerge and wave.
The clamour then abruptly stops
And everyone looks grave.

There is no band, no interview,
No banner "Welcome back".
And twenty men surround the crew
In uniform of black.

Their leader says "Arrest this crew
And hold them in the gaol,
And keep them constantly in view.
They'll not be granted bail.

Your trial begins on Monday week,
You'll have ten days of peace.
Your outlook is extremely bleak
For we're the Language Police."

The ten days passed, they came to court,
The charge was Word Abuse,
Or "Using Words With Little Thought
And Even Less Excuse."

And so began the famous trial:
The crew stood in the dock
And tried to launch a strong denial,
Especially Mr Spock.

The Prosecutor, short and dark,
A fiery little man,
Said "Did you make that trite remark
In setting out your plan?

32

Part 1: STORIES & BALLADS

Now, did you say you'd been to Mars
And so this time you planned
'To boldly go' among the stars
Then, ten years later, land?"

One witness, two, and then a third
Persuasively agreed
They'd clearly heard each damning word,
What use was there to plead?

It took the jury half an hour
Their verdict to bring in:
The Foreman with a baleful glower
Said "Guilty of the sin."

The Judge said "For this dreadful crime
A lesson I must teach.
In prison you will spend your time.
That's fifteen years for each."

They pleaded hard, but all in vain:
The world would not forgive
That writers' pain, that pedants' bane
The split infinitive!

That happened years ahead, don't fret,
The crew will earn release.
But ... pity we don't have them, yet,
Those lovely Language Police!

The COMPLETE WIT & WHIMSEY

In the late 1980's I hit upon the idea of updating a few fairy stories and putting them into verse. "Cinderella" was the was the first story to get the treatment. It was only a few years later that I found, to my chagrin, that some fellow called Roald Dahl had done exactly the same thing. I've read some of his books to my grandchildren, but I've never read his converted fairy stories, probably becauseI'm frightened of finding they're much better than my own efforts!

A WHOLE NEW BALL GAME

I

In a mansion somewhat grotty
Lived two sisters large and spotty
With their silly widowed mother
Who, late in life, had wed another -
A baron who (and here's the pity)
Had lost his fortune in the city,
And to his second marriage brought a
Young, attractive, teenage daughter
And a winsome little valet:
That completes the ménage tally.

II

The Ugly sisters, pushing thirty,
Shunned all household duties dirty
And shoved their step-sister about
With many a scream and many a clout
Till finally, with lots of bitching
Banished her down to the kitchen
With the little valet feller,
Buttons he - she Cinderella.
The sisters kept them on the hop
And made them work till fit to drop.

III

One day arrived an invitation
That caused no little consternation:
There was to be a Royal Ball
And they were summoned - one and all.
Sweet Cinderella felt elated
Until the sisters that she hated
Caused unspeakable distress
By saying "As you're such a mess
You cannot go, you'll stay behind
And scrub!" They really were unkind.
And then the sisters rushed to town
To purchase each a frothy gown.

IV

At last the magic night arrived,
The sisters dressed, and each contrived
To look less like a pink gorilla
With perfumes, creams and Polyfilla.
Then off they went, as Cinders crept
Upstairs to see them go, and wept,
Till Buttons said "Cheer up, my dear,
Let's go and have a crafty beer."
(I know I shouldn't really blab it,
But swigging booze was Buttons' habit.)

V

Then suddenly in radiant light
A lovely lady all in white
Appeared and said to Cinders "Hi!
You shall go to the Ball, for I
Am Fairy Godmother to you
And here's exactly what to do ...."
They quickly found some rats and mice
And pumpkin large, then in a trice
A coach appeared with horses four
And footmen standing by the door.
Dear Cinders clapped her hands in glee
And said "That's great, but look at me.
I can't go to a function royal

Part 1: STORIES & BALLADS

In dirty rags that stink of oil."
"Stand still, my dear" the Fairy said,
Then suddenly from toe to head
Cinderella was attired
In everything that was required:
A gown with sequins quite replete
And crystal slippers for her feet
And even (sparing no expenses)
Lingerie from Marks and Spencers.

VI

As Cinders climbed into her coach
Buttons voiced a strong reproach:
"Can't I go there and join the fun?"
The Fairy said "I'm sorry, son"
She sadly shook her thick blonde curls,
"My magic only works for girls,"
Then said "Now Cinders, pay attention,
There's one thing I forgot to mention:
The spell wears off at midnight's chime,
So keep a good eye on the time,
For after that all things revert
To what they were, so be alert.
Now off you go and stun them all,
Good-bye, my dear, and have a ball!"
Then, as these words the Fairy spoke,
She vanished in a puff of smoke.

VII

As Cinders' coach rolled through the gate
Poor Buttons sadly cursed his fate.
He'd love to go to somewhere posh
With fancy girls and fancy nosh.
Silently he shed a tear,
Then went and had another beer,
And then he had a couple more,
Then lay down and began to snore.

VIII

Festivities were in full flow
As Cinderella, with a slow
And measured step, her entrance made
And put all others in the shade.
Three hundred guests just stood and stared,
The younger ladies simply glared
As Cinders, all serene in chinz,
Glided slowly to the Prince,
And he, in uniform, so dashing
Cried "I say, you do look smashing!
A veritable little treasure.
But come, my dear, let's tread a measure.
You'll dance with no-one else, my beauty."
She murmured "Yes, Sire, that's my duty."
And so they danced the night away
Like little children out to play:
Foxtrots, Quicksteps, wild Fandangos,
Waltzes, Sambas, Polkas, Tangos,
To music pop and music folky
(They even did the Hokey-Cokey),
While Cinders' sisters to their pals
Said "No look-in for us, you gals.
He won't want mutton when there's lamb,
But really we don't give a damn."
With overt yawn and overt stifle
They went back to their cream and trifle.

IX

Then Cinders, memory now dawning
Of the Fairy's sombre warning
Said "Leaving you would be a crime,
But can you tell me, Sire, the time?"
The Prince said "It's not very late,
It's just 11.58."
"Oh!" screamed Cinders, "I must fly,
Sorry, I must say good-bye,
I really wish I could avoid it,
But thank you, Sire, I have enjoyed it!"
With that she raced across the floor
And nipped out through the ballroom door.

The COMPLETE WIT & WHIMSEY

The Prince just stood there, thunder-struck,
And thought "What jolly rotten luck!"

X

So Cinderella from the ball
Came fleeing, nearly had a fall,
Just made it to the coach in time
As midnight bells began to chime.
Then, as she sat back in her mink,
Her flunkies all began to shrink;
And, as she snuggled in her ermine,
It turned into a bunch of vermin.
Then gradually her golden coach,
As transformation did encroach,
Became again a pumpkin squishy,
While Cinderella, once so dishy,
Found herself reduced as quick as
Lightening to her bra and knickers,
And, as she shed her final zipper,
Yelled "I've lost a flipping slipper!"
She limped back home and, feeling glum
And frozen, had a tot of rum.
Then friendly Buttons tucked her in
And, for a night-cap, had a gin.

XI

Next day a Royal Proclamation
In the household caused sensation:
The Prince had found a shoe of crystal
In his palace (just near Bristol):
Whosever foot the slipper fitted
Was the maiden who had flitted.
When he found her, they would wed
And occupy the Royal Bed.

XII

At last the Royal entourage
Reached Cinders' mansion, where a large
And handsome footman came inside
To look for the prospective bride,
While in the background stood the Prince,
Slowly sucking Polo mints.
The Ugly Sisters, all aglow,
Said "Come on, mate, let's have a go."
The one built like a Rugby prop
Squeezed and squeezed, but had to stop.
The other one (with the moustache)
Also found it quite a squash.
"It's only 'cos we've both got blisters"
Glumly whined the Ugly Sisters.

XIII

The footman asked "Who else lives here?"
Then little Buttons did appear.
"There's Cinderella, Sir" he said,
"She's in the kitchen, making bread,
And doing other bits of cooking.
To tell the truth she's quite good looking."
The sisters screamed "That little slut!
They might as well try you, you mutt."
The footman faced them both and bowed,
"Gentlemen are not allowed.
We cannot try it on a feller.
Now, where's this girl called Cinderella?"

XIV

As she heard him say the name
'Cinderella' - in she came.
Although she'd just been slicing bacon
Her beauty could not be mistaken.
She sat upon a stool and put
The dainty slipper on her foot,
And when it fitted like a glove,
The Prince cried "I have found my love.
You surely are the maid I seek,"
And kissed her lightly on the cheek.
"Come to the palace right away,
For we must plan our wedding day.

Part 1: STORIES & BALLADS

So go and pack a little case
With clothes, and powder for your face
And shampoo for your lovely hair."
"I haven't anything to wear"
Forlornly Cinderella said,
Then found herself from toe to head
Apparelled in the clothes she wore
To the ball the night before.

XV

The Prince said "Come on, don't be daft,
You're beautifully dressed and coiffed."
He said to Buttons "You come, too
To help prepare the wedding do,"
Then, turning to the sisters, cried
"I need you both to help the bride.
I'm sure at this you'll be ecstatic -
You'll have a small room in the attic."
The sisters purred "Oh, what an honour,
We'll gladly come and wait upon her.
We'd like to help your footmen, too.
We're sure they've got a lot to do."
(They weren't so dumb, this ugly pair:
They knew the footmen that worked there
Were gorgeous hunks with lots of
　　muscles.
It sent a thrill right through their bustles.)

XVI

And so the Prince and Cinders wed
And occupied the Royal Bed.
The sisters now are Maids-in Waiting,
And both of them are contemplating
Marriage, for they're going steady
With two footmen, Sid and Eddie,
While Buttons is the butler now.
He's sworn off drink - and kept his vow.
Let's hope he has this battle won
And Buttons never comes undone!

The COMPLETE WIT & WHIMSEY

Here is another fairy story converted into verse

THE FROG PRINCE

I

Hark while this tale I now unfold:
A princess lovely to behold
Lived in a castle large and splendid
'Mid gardens beautifully tended.
Each morning she would take a stroll
The wond'rous gardens to extol:
She was particularly fond
Of dreaming by the lily pond:
When would a prince on charger white
Ride up to her, his troth to plight?
Were those the words? (she felt pedantic)
Well, something like that, quite romantic.
When would he come and make her swoon
Like they did in Mills and Boon?

II

One day as she stood musing there
A plopping noise gave her a scare,
And as she turned round, feeling nervous,
A little frog came to the surface.
"Good morning, Princess" said the frog.
The Princess stared at him, agog.
"But you can talk!" she cried in awe.
The frog said "Yes, I can. What's more
I'm really not a frog at all,
I am a Prince who's strong and tall.
A wicked witch has cast a spell,
Made me a frog, so here I dwell
Among the lilies of this pond and
Feeling really quite despondent."

III

"Oh, Mr Frog" the Princess cried,
"Cannot this deed be rectified?"
The frog replied "Well, yes it can.
I can be turned into a man,
But only with a kiss or two
From a Princess just like you.
Not here of course, it wouldn't work:
In your bedroom I must lurk,
Then later, when you go to bed
I'll pop up somewhere near your head.
And when you've showered me with kisses
I'll be a Prince, you'll be my missus."
"I'll do it, frog" the Princess cried
"So jump up here and have a ride."
And so this odd-assorted twosome
(The frog tucked snugly in her bosom)
To the palace made their way
And waited till the end of day.

IV

"Goodnights" having all been said,
The Princess made her way to bed
And thought "How strange, a frog I'm dating."
Then when the royal Maids-in-Waiting
Had washed her face and brushed her curls,
She gracefully dismissed the girls.
Then as her head the pillow touched
A slimy hand her shoulder clutched.
The frog appeared, said "Did you miss me?
But now has come the time to kiss me!"
Although repelled, the lovely Princess
With sundry shudderings and winces
Grabbed the slippery little beast
And kissed him twenty times at least.
Then suddenly, with lightening flashing,
A young man handsome, strong and dashing

Part 1: STORIES & BALLADS

Stood upon the bedroom floor.
The little frog? He was no more.

V
Next morning, when the Upstairs Maid
Brought the toast and marmalade,
Some coffee and the Telegraph,
She gave a wink, she gave a laugh:
"Oh Mistress, what a lovely lad,
Just wait until I tell your Dad."
She disappeared, and seconds later
Came the King, the royal pater.
He saw the Princess, saw the Prince,
His royal words he did not mince.
He said "Young man, how very rude you are
To sneak into my daughter's boudoir.
The penalty is sudden death,
Prepare to take your final breath."
But as the King began to leave,
The Princess clutched him by the sleeve.
"Papa" she cried, "Don't act in haste.
I'm still comparatively chaste.
We only had a little snog
And that was when he was a frog.
He's now a Prince, we wish to wed;
We can't do that if he is dead."

VI
Then all at once there came a roar,
And rushing through the bedroom door
They saw a bent and hideous hag,
Who stank enough to make them gag.
"Your Majesty" the old crone said,
"No need to chop off this lad's head,
For I can wave my wand, and then
He'll turn into a frog again."
The King thought 'Perhaps I'm too doctrinal,
Killing tends to be quite final,
But I must set some sort of tone
For actions that I can't condone.

This hag I see before my eyes
Is offering a compromise.'
"Oh, very well" the King declared,
"Make him a frog. His life is spared."

VII
Three times she waved her wand. Anon
A frog appeared, the Prince was gone.
But something happened to her magic
Anthropomorphically tragic:
Not just one frog, but two appeared.
The witch said "Ah, it's as I feared,
The girl was standing in the spell
So she's become a frog as well.
But just to show my sense of fun
I'll charge you only for the one.
No, don't pay now, I'll see you later."
Then, reaching for her calculator,
Said "Prince to frog, the largest spell,
With Sunday overtime as well,
And service charge, now then let's see,
That's fifty quid, plus VAT."
The King roared "You must be insane,
Turn my daughter back again!"
"I can't" she leered, without remorse,
"I've only done the basic course.
Men are easy, either way,
But not so girls, a frog she'll stay."
"Then you shall die - off with her head!"
And soldiers rushed in 'ere she fled
To drag her off, her head to dock
Upon the royal chopping block.

VIII
The King wept "Oh, my darling daughter,
I'll have to put you in some water.
Your suitor, too, the noble Prince,
He shall go with you, daughter, since
He loved you true, and you loved him.
Henceforth together you shall swim.
To the pond you both shall come.
It's all right, love, I'll tell your Mum."
So tenderly, with utmost care
To the pond he bore the pair

And gently placed them in the water,
Erstwhile Prince and erstwhile daughter.
But, as he did, there came a scream
From the royal guillotine,
Then, as the frogs sank to the mud,
There came a rather nasty thud:
They'd killed the witch, destroyed her wand.

IX

Meanwhile, at the lily pond,
Some curious events began
A maiden surfaced, then a man.
The witch's death had smashed the spell.
The Princess yelled "Now swim like hell!"
"I can't!" the Prince cried, going down,
"I never learned, I'm going to drown!"
The Princess gasped "No, no, your head'll
Not go down, I've got a medal,
Lives from drowning I can save
So hold on tight and just be brave."
With that she heaved the Prince's chest
On to her ample, soggy breast
And to the nearest bit of shore
Her charming Prince she gamely bore.

X

They soon were wed midst joy and laughter,
And not so many months thereafter
On a splendid summer's morn
A lovely babe to them was born.
The Princess, overcome with joy
Said "What a darling little boy.
My happiness is now complete,
He'll be a swimmer - see those feet!"

Part 1: STORIES & BALLADS

Another of my fairy-story make-overs.

THE KING'S INCREDIBLE LIGHTWEIGHT ROBES

I

In mediæval times, they say,
In a country far away
There lived a King in manner grand,
Greatly feared throughout the land.
He treated everyone like fools.
His word was law, he made the rules,
And anyone who disobeyed
With his life untimely paid.
Totally obsessed with vanity,
The King was verging on insanity,
Not yet quite mad, and not eccentric -
Just absolutely egocentric.
(He even made them write an opera
To indulge his *amour propre*.)

II

One day his Ministers he summoned:
"OK you lot," he said, "Just come and
Hear my latest Royal Decree."
They listened, all on bended knee.
"In three months time" he said with verve
"A grand occasion we'll observe:
The Jubilee of my accession,
And I must make a good impression.
To my subjects I'll appear
Decked out in the finest gear.
There'll be, of course, a Grand Parade,
And ice-cream, buns and lemonade.
We'll ask a host of foreign dignatories,
Kings and treaty signatories.
There'll be some bands and all that
    action,
But naturally, the star attraction
Will be me in all my glory.
In years to come they'll tell the story
Of this day. And best of all -
The highlight of the Festival -
The Royal Robes, the King's Attire!
The consequences will be dire
If you cannot find for me
The finest tailor that there be:
A man of flair, a craftsman pure,
Practitioner of *haute-couture*,
A man of unsurpassing skill
To rig me out - and hang the bill!
So get to work, achieve this goal
Or, mark my words, some heads will roll!"
The King departed with a flourish,
Leaving Ministers to nourish
This, his latest proclamation
In a state of consternation.

III

They drew up plans. Within a week
'Twas widely known they wished to seek
A tailor that could dress the King
In robes as posh as anything.
Then quickly to the palace door
Flocked skilful tailors by the score
To try each one his wares to sell
And make the King a proper swell,
From China, Rome and Aberdeen
With flannel, silk and gabardine.
But no-one would the King enlist:
All were disdainfully dismissed.

IV

The Ministers in trepidation
Of corporate decapitation
Wondered where there lived a tailor
To save them from the axeman-gaolor,
Until one day a handsome fellow
In suit of blue and shirt of yellow
Drove up to the palace door
In a splendid coach and four.

The COMPLETE WIT & WHIMSEY

He gave the Ministers a glare
And said "Bonjour, I'm M'sieur Pierre.
I've brought my latest Spring Collection
For His Majesty's inspection."
He handed them his business card.
They led him past the Palace Guard
Through endless corridors of gloom
Unto the Royal Dressing Room,
Bearing with them one large trunk
Full, no doubt, of tailor's junk.
Then M'sieur Pierre in haughty tone
Said "I must see the King alone.
My secrets I refuse to share
With any but the King - so there!"
He gave a toot upon a horn,
The King appeared and gave a yawn,
Then, when he saw the garish tailor
Said "Well I never, hello sailor.
But come on in, that's all I ask
If you are equal to the task."
So, confidently M'sieur Pierre
Strode in to show the King his ware.

V

"The robes that I have brought for you
Are fashioned in the richest hue
Of silk as fine as thistledown,
Quite weightless. Sire, remove your crown
And try them on. You'll be amazed
How light they are, and when you've gazed
At what a splendid sight you are -
The noblest King there is by far -
You'll smile at me most gratefully
And pay my quite outrageous fee."

VI

The King found M'sieur Pierre most charming -
A trifle bold, but quite disarming.
"Show me, show me, man," he said.
The trunk was opened, and instead
Of robes, the King saw nothing much.
Said M'sieur Pierre "Now just you touch
This wispy, gossamer material,
So insubstantial, so ethereal."
The King thought, feeling rather small,
"There's something in there, after all."
"Yes, yes" he cried, "They're really grand,
The finest robes in all the land.
I'll try them on from head to feet."
The tailor smiled at his conceit.
The King immediately undressed
And M'sieur Pierre, at his behest,
Helped him don each precious robe,
While the King with pleasure glowed.
Then M'sieur Pierre, with loud applause,
Said "Let me call these slaves of yours.
I'm sure you'll value their opinions."
He summoned in the Royal minions
And whispered "Right, your heads won't roll
If you will heartily extol
The Royal robes - you get my meaning?"
They saw the King, stark naked, preening.

VII

"Well, how d'you like this flimsy gear?
Your opinion I must hear."
"Oh, Sire" they minced "You look a treat
From Royal head to Royal feet!"
To please the King they were quite frantic
And sickeningly sycophantic.
Said M'sieur Pierre with great elation
"They need a minor alteration.
I'll take the robes with me" said he
"And come back for your Jubilee,
When I will help you, Sire, to dress
Your many subjects to impress.
My bill? I've not the faintest notion,
Let's call it half a million groschen.
Here, let me help you to disrobe."

Part 1: STORIES & BALLADS

The clothes into the trunk he stowed
And left them standing somewhat speechless,
The King, of course, remaining breechless.

VIII

The Ministers, alone, conferred,
Agreed they would not say a word.
"He's conned the King, that's quite apparent
(Or should one say it's quite transparent?)
To tell the King we would be dumb.
We've saved our necks, so let's keep mum."

IX

The Great Day dawned, the crowds appeared
Because the King was greatly feared.
In little groups they stood there mute
Along the Royal procession route.
They loathed parades, so stood there sullen
Expecting just another dull 'un.

X

Meanwhile, M'sieur Pierre returned
(In view of all the cash he'd earned),
And put to practice all his art
To make the King look nice and smart;
And Ministers all bobbed about
In case the King had any doubt,
Telling him he looked superb
And all the usual fawning blurb.

XI

At last began the Grand Parade
Headed by a cavalcade
Of Royal Guards on snow-white stallions
Bedecked with ribbons and medallions.
Then came the bands with fife and drum.
There were no cheers, the crowd was dumb.
Next came by a dozen carriages
Of children from the Royal marriages,
And twenty foreign dignitaries
And thirty treaty signatories.
Then lastly from the palace rolled
The King's own coach of purest gold,
And in the coach the King stood proud
Inviting homage from the crowd,
Who smiled and whispered "This is rude,
The King's completely in the nude."
But, though the King looked quite absurd,
No-one dared to breathe a word.
To do so would have led to death,
So, though they smiled, they held their breath,
Until a little eight-year-old
Shouted out, so brave, so bold
"I think the King looks very silly
'Cause I can see the Royal Willy!"

XII

The crowd erupted with a roar
And gave a communal guffaw.
Then all began to chant and shout
The words the boy had blurted out:
"We think the King looks very silly
'Cause we can see the Royal Willy!
We think the King looks very silly
'Cause we can see the Royal Willy!"
The King stood cowering in his coach
As he saw the crowd approach,
And heard the most salacious paeon
From voices utterly plebian.
Upon the route they did encroach
And shook the Royal golden coach.

XIII

"Save me, Guards!" the King implored,
"And you shall have a rich reward.
Throw these wretches into gaol!"

The King was very, very pale.
With perspiration he was soaking.
"Ten thousand serfs? You must be
   joking!"
Said the Captain of the Guard,
"I'm sorry, Sire, it's no holds barred;
And anyway, the crowd is right,
You really look a dreadful sight.
The Guards agree, you do look silly
Showing off the Royal Willy.
I'll save you, if it's not too late
If you agree to abdicate.
For if you don't, you'll feel the pinch,
I'm sure this mob is out to lynch."

XIV

The King exclaimed "I will, I will,
Fetch me parchment and a quill."
He wrote, emitting one loud groan,
"I, King, hereby renounce my throne."
Then, with the paper in his hand,
Signed by the ruler of the land,
The Captain strode off for to seek
The topmost judge, the Royal Beak,
Who said "Yes, there's no doubt it's legal,
It is an abdication regal."
At last the King, by Guards protected,
And feeling very much dejected,
Was brought back to his Royal home,
Then exiled, somewhere south of Rome,
Together with the Royal wives
And children, thankful for their lives.

XV

With his exile came the birth
Of an era filled with mirth.
The land with happiness did ring
Now governed by another King.
All the people were well fed,
Each with roof above his head.
And everyone was smartly dressed
At Royal expense. I'm sure you've
   guessed
The man they crowned with joyful cries:
The author of the King's demise,
The man in *haute-couture* well versed,
Yes, M'sieur Pierre - King Pierre the First!

Part 1: STORIES & BALLADS

This poem recalls all those visits I made, in the course of duty, to Whitehall, to attend meetings with London-based civil servants, whose numbers included representatives from the Foreign and Commonwealth Office (FCO.) I wrote this just before the National Lottery was launched, when winning the pools was still the big fantasy.

FOSDYKE OF THE FCO

I

Fosdyke of the FCO
From his window gazed below.
He saw the crowds in Whitehall milling,
Pretty humdrum - yet so thrilling:
'They are free while I am caged'
That wicked voice within him raged.
(He thought he heard a mocking laugh
From somewhere near the Cenotaph).
He eyed his tray - a daunting pile
Then sighed, and seized the topmost file.

II

In strode Hallam, eyes ablaze
And fixed him with unflinching gaze.
"Where the hell's your damned report?"
And Fosdyke, poised for smart retort,
Thought better of it and, instead,
"It's not quite finished, Sir," he said.
He called him "Sir" - he was quite senior,
"There's just a bit to add on Kenya."
"Well, hurry man, I need it soon,
By two o'clock this afternoon.
And by the way, Department Head
Is going walkies" Hallam said,
"A conference in Singapore,
He needs a brief by half past four."
His voice had risen to a shout,
"So Fosdyke, get your finger out!"
Then Hallam breezed back out again
And Fosdyke, with a look of pain,
Put head in hands and sadly sighed.
He wished the fairies would provide
A Rumpelstiltskin who could spin

Facts into reports for him.
But, summoning his concentration,
With coffee black, and perspiration,
He did his task, and did it well
And Hallam? He could go to hell.
So Fosdyke plodded home to dinner
To his haven, south of Pinner,
Where his kids and lovely wife
Comprised the happy side of life.

III

The weekend came, a bright oasis:
The Fosdyke tribe, with smiling faces
Set about the family chores,
Shopping, mowing, painting doors.
Then, as the kids the Escort hosed
In his armchair Fosdyke dozed
(That was within the family rules),
Then later on, he'd check his pools.

IV

While Mrs Fosdyke busily
Made preparations for their tea,
And Fosdyke dreamed of lots of fun
In foreign climes, beneath the sun
For three small kids and two adults,
A voice said "Classified Results".
He left his dream somewhere near Cairo
And jumped awake and grabbed his biro;
And as his missus put the soup on
He quickly found his football coupon.
Then, as the one-all draws he counted,
Excitement in him slowly mounted,

The COMPLETE WIT & WHIMSEY

Till finally he knew his fate:
Of eight such draws, he'd picked all eight!
He thought "I won't let on just yet
That we will never be in debt.
I'll wait until the cheque arrives
And give the wife a nice surprise.
To tell her now, I'd be a crackpot
Especially if it's not a jackpot."

V

The family sat down to tea
And Fosdyke junior, saucily,
Said "Why is Daddy smiling so?
Daddy, please, I'd like to know."
Then Fosdyke tertius, with a whoop
Said "Daddy's spilled his mushroom soup!"
"Now don't be cheeky" said his Dad,
"No story-time for you, my lad."
That was, of course, an idle threat,
For three young Fosdykes dripping wet,
Emerging from their nightly bath
Heard Daddy give a little laugh;
And, as he patted them quite dry,
He gave a look a trifle sly
And said "Now hurry into bed,"
Then took a story-book and read.
A wond'rous tale their father told
Of straw that could be spun to gold.

VI

On Monday morning, with a glower,
In the corridors of power,
Hallam muttered "Fosdyke's late in,
That little swine has kept me waiting!"
(He'd had a weekend rather boozie
With an energetic floozie).
Then finally, at 0920,
Fosdyke entered, humming gently.
Hallam growled "I don't believe
You said you'd have a half-day's leave.

But now you're here, there's work to do:
A rather difficult PQ:
A Parliamentary Question, son,
So that should give you lots of fun!"
He hurled a file at Fosdyke's chest,
"Now get stuck in, no time to rest."
Fosdyke thought "Right, here's my chance."
He gave the file the merest glance
And, tossing it upon a shelf,
Said "Do the bloody thing yourself
And get it right for goodness sake.
Now clear off - it's my coffee break!"

VII

Hallam's face went deathly white.
He slowly breathed "Did I hear right?"
He turned and stormed out cursing "Well,
I'm taking this to Personnel!
You've really come a proper Burton.
You're for the high-jump, that's for certain."
Said Fosdyke "Well, that's fine by me.
I've had this little legacy.
No longer must I slave for you,
I'll just resign - and up yours, too!"
Hallam gasped in consternation
At Fosdyke's insubordination
Then hurried off to Personnel
To see they gave young Fosdyke hell.
And Fosdyke dreamed the day away
Toying with his Pending Tray.

VIII

That evening, kids all safe in bed,
Holiday brochures he read.
Several happy hours he killed
(His wife was at the Womens' Guild).
Something special he would choose,
Like a Caribbean cruise -
The children might not like that, though.
The country for a month or so

Part 1: STORIES & BALLADS

Might be an even better bet,
Ah, yes now, 'Cottages to Let' -
Here's a nice one outside Truro.

IX

His idle gaze fell on the bureau,
And what he saw there made him gape:
A thing rectangular in shape
And white in colour, near the lamp,
Complete with first-class postage stamp:
Last week's entry on the Pools
Still sitting there. Of all the fools
He took the prize. His dream was over,
No holiday, no Merc or Rover.
The disappointment of his life!
(Thank God he hadn't told his wife).
Worse still, at work he'd pitched the line
To Hallam that he would resign.
But then, of course, they might just sack him
For gross misconduct - send him packing.

X

His wife returned, all bright and happy:
"We had a talk, this travel chappy
Spoke about exotic cruises,
Seems to me they're just for losers,
All the failures of life
After someone else's wife,
And women, too, they're just the same,
Totally devoid of shame.
What's up my love, you look quite dead.
Let's have some tea and go to bed."

XI

As he arrived at work next day
He found a message in his tray:
Personnel would like a chat
At twelve o'clock. "Oh, well that's that.
They're going to read the Riot Act,
Will I escape, career intact?"

Poor Fosdyke felt extremely low
And thought the darkest thoughts, although
One feature of the day was bright:
Hallam had kept out of sight.

XII

To Personnel at stroke of noon
Reported Fosdyke. Very soon
They bade him enter. He obeyed.
An older man of Hallam's grade
Said "Sorry that we've dragged you here
But something has come up, I fear.
Hallam, whom you know, of course,
Represents a rare resource:
Not the easiest of chaps,
But quite an expert on the Japs.
We've got this treaty thing, so he,
Seconded temporarily,
Will bring his expertise to bear,
To get the wording fair and square.
In any case, this Staff Inspection
Recommends we close his Section."
He waved a paper in the air.
"Well, anyway, it's all in there.
So, what of you? Well, truth to tell
We're rather short in Personnel,
So if you'd like to, please report
For duties here. Give it some thought.
And let me know by close of play."

XIII

For the remainder of the day
Our hero, very much elated,
Mothballed all those files he hated,
And chatted up a girl with dark eyes,
Second-in-command at Archives.
At five he 'phoned up Personnel,
Confirmed he'd join them - what the hell!

XIV

Just one year later, Fosdyke's boss
Said "Well, our gain is Hallam's loss:
Ambassadors and H of C's,
Deployment with the greatest ease,
The best man we could get in Lagos,
Hallam to the Turks and Caicos;
The postings that have been required
All sanctioned, every one inspired,
And all of this is down to you.
Promotion, long since overdue,
Has come, so if you've no objection,
We'd like you now to run the Section.
Then, when you feel you're getting bored,
We'll find you something nice abroad."

XV

Thus, Fosdyke launched his Great Career:
Promotion almost every year.
With posts in Paris, Bonn and Rome
And complex duties back at home,
With stints of this and stints of that
Emerged a skilful diplomat,
Darling of the cocktail circuit.
(The system - he knew how to work it:
But then he'd learned the system well,
When Section Head in Personnel).
He picked up gongs, of course, eg
CBE, KCMG,
In twenty years, no more, no less
He ended up as P.U.S.*
While Hallam now, without demur,
Works hard for him and calls him 'Sir'.

* Permanent Under-Secretary

Part 1: STORIES & BALLADS

Although I wrote this in about 1993, some of the features of supermarket shopping remain just as valid today. For those which have changed, this story can be regarded as a piece of history. As a work of art, the poem has little to commend it – it's just a piece of doggerel: but isn't that exactly the style needed for the theme – the shoddy treatment of customers?

TALKING SHOP

I

The Annual Convention
 Is held each year in Kent.
They travel here from far and near
To grace the grand event:
Supermarket managers,
At least 500 strong
Reach their target outside Margate -
What a noisy throng!
"British United Merchants"
The platform banner reads
(The B.U.M. - you won't know them:
But what about their deeds!)

II

 Let's eavesdrop on this meeting:
The Chairman speaks: "My friends,
We're here, of course, (and here in force)
To look at recent trends
And then reveal the winner
Of this year's Silver Cup
For new ideas (as Christmas nears)
To mess the shopper up!"
The members of the B.U.M.
Their loud approval roar,
And many stand and wave a hand
And stamp upon the floor.

III

The Chairman says "Remember
The effort that it takes
To irritate the ones we hate"
(His voice with passion shakes)

"The cruel, unthinking public,
Who desecrate our stores,
Who spoil all day each neat display
And smear our shiny floors!
The shoppers need us, we need them -
We can't, of course desert them:
What we must do, each year anew,
Is find new ways to hurt them!"

The delegates all fall about,
They laugh and roll their eyes.
With huge guffaws some break their jaws
And others bruise their thighs.

IV

 "Right, simmer down and let's proceed",
The Chairman says at last.
"And let us first review the worst
Of deeds done in the past."
He looks around the audience:
"Where's Ashley Briggs from Leek?"
"I'm here" he cries, with sparkling eyes,
And leaps on stage to speak.
"We were the first to target thirst,
And milk we thought we'd start on.
We made the spout that won't come out
And stays glued to the carton!"

The delegates all fall about,
They laugh and roll their eyes.
With huge guffaws, some break their jaws
And others bruise their thighs.

The COMPLETE WIT & WHIMSEY

V

Up jumps a man from Wigan,
Who gives a knowing leer.
"We won the cup by thinking up
That famous trick with beer.
We wanted customers to think
'These shops are out to cheat us',
And so we put the price in pints
And quantities in litres.
We also had this soft drink -
Well, nobody would buy it
Until we lit upon a hit:
A label that said 'Diet'"

The delegates all fall about,
They laugh and roll their eyes.
With huge guffaws some break their jaws
And others bruise their thighs.

VI

Then, next a well-groomed lady
In tailored suit of beige
Walks down the aisle, and with a smile
Climbs briskly on the stage.
She says "What things break easily,
What things are very brittle?"
And from the floor there comes a roar:
"Biscuits big and little!"
"Right. That's why biscuit wrapping is
The flimsiest they make,
So some will crack in every pack
And half of them will break!"

The delegates all fall about
They laugh and roll their eyes.
With huge guffaws some break their jaws
And others bruise their thighs.

VII

The next to speak is far from meek -
A manager named Sam -
His voice is tough: "There's loads of stuff,
Like bacon, cheese and ham,
We now seal tight with all our might
In little plastic cases,
With utmost care expel the air
Now see the shoppers' faces!
There's no way they can open them -
It needs enormous power.
I tell no lies", he loudly cries,
"That was our finest hour!"

The delegates all fall about,
They laugh and roll their eyes.
With huge guffaws some break their jaws
And others bruise their thighs.

VIII

Then on the stage walks Henry Sage,
Who used to be a vet.
Their eyes he meets, and then he bleats
"You ain't heard nothing yet!
We made that bag with stitching on,
For pet-food mix and such:
A useful thing, just pull the string,
It opens at a touch.
Of course it won't, and why is this?"
(He bangs hard with the gavel),
"The string has got an extra knot
So that it can't unravel!"

The delegates all fall about
They laugh and roll their eyes.
With huge guffaws some break their jaws
And others bruise their thighs.

IX

The chairman says "I'll take one more.
Now who is it to be?"
A girl called Clare with bright red hair

Part 1: STORIES & BALLADS

Says "Right then, make it me.
We forced the customer to buy
Eight batteries for his clocks,
Four bulbs for lights, three pairs of tights
And umpteen pairs of socks.
These extra few - what will they do?
When all they need is one?
The shopper's cross, his gain's his loss,
Which adds to all the fun!"

The delegates all fall about,
They laugh and roll their eyes.
With huge guffaws some break their jaws
And others bruise their thighs.

X

The Chairman cries "Now, this year's prize -
Who's won the Silver Cup
For new ideas (as Christmas nears)
To mess the shopper up?
The B.U.M. are proud to welcome
To this great occasion
A man who cares. The man who chairs
That fine Association
Of Retail Sales Executives -
Our splendid parent Union"
They give a cheer, athirst to hear
The eminent Mancunian.

XI

"My friends," said he, "A.R.S.E.
Applauds the B.U.M."
(He gamely gropes three envelopes)
"From whom these ideas stem.
In Third Place is the sticky tag
For putting names on apples -
The shopper weeps, it's there for keeps
However hard he grapples.
Because it's made with Superglue
No fingers can defeat it,
So he must slice it to excise it,
 - Else he has to eat it.

The delegates all fall about
They laugh and roll their eyes.
With huge guffaws some break their jaws
And others bruise their thighs.

XII

"In second place, we've got this case
Designed to carry eggs.
It's got this top, a proper flop,
Secured by little pegs.
The shoppers will be really fooled,
They'll think 'What great protection.'
In point of fact, the way they're packed
Won't bear a close inspection.
The reinforcement on the lid
Is really just a token,
And when they get them home they fret
Because they're mostly broken."

The delegates all fall about,
They laugh and roll their eyes.
With huge guffaws some break their jaws
And others bruise their thighs.

XIII

"And finally" the V.I.P.
Says, "Number One this Year"
(Necks are craned and ears are strained
So delegates can hear)
"The UK Supertrolley
Let's call a spade a spade:
It's brash, it's flash, it's utter trash,
What's more, it's British made.
But let us hear more detail
From the man who made this jewel:
As engineer he has no peer:
He's Percy Pain from Poole!"

XIV

A tiny, oldish fellow
In chocolate corduroys
Leaps on the stage, despite his age,
Amid a sea of noise.
The Chairman calls for order
As the din is so intense,
Then Percy speaks and sucks his
    cheeks,
Recalling past events:
"Approaching thirty years ago
A trolley we designed
To use in stores for shopping chores -
The first one of its kind.

XV

We used a special formula
And made the thing in sections
With (as you know) those wheels that go
In opposite directions.
Our latest model barely moves
I'm happy to proclaim:
And all is due to this computer
Underneath the frame.
The customers will curse their fate,
They couldn't have a worse year:
Because, you see, we guarantee
Both chaos and inertia!"

The delegates all fall about,
They laugh and roll their eyes.
With huge guffaws some break their jaws
And others bruise their thighs.

XVI

And now the Meeting's over,
The delegates disband
To plan, and think of food and drink
Of every make and brand,
And how they'll meet the challenge
That the year ahead presents
To irritate that reprobate
Each manager resents:
The cruel, unthinking shopper,
Who desecrates the stores
And spoils all day each neat display,
And smears the shiny floors.

PART 2: In Lightest Vein

Can you remember the first time you fell in love or had a hopeless crush on someone? In the 1940's and 1950's I went to an all-male grammar school - all boys and all men teachers, until one amazing day, after one of the teachers had retired, his replacement arrived and it was a lady teacher. And not just a lady teacher, but a young and very pretty lady teacher. You can imagine the effect this had on the school. Several hundred spotty youths would fall over each other to open the door for her or carry her books. Here's a poem that recalls for me those days. It's about the hopeless passion felt by an adolescent lad for his lady teacher - in this case his Maths teacher. The poem is called "CRUSH".

CRUSH

Oh, dear Miss Phillips, spare a thought
For those you teach and those you
    taught.
Delicious mathematics mentor,
Guide, instructor, sweet tormentor,
Charming me with flawless features
Ne'er before bestowed on teachers:
Spheres of blue 'neath congruent brows,
Where Thought his faultless furrow
    ploughs,
And perfect nose, isoscelean,
Urge from me this reckless paean.
Lips that laugh in carmine curves
Erode the sinews, pluck the nerves.
To kiss them would that I had dared
When last they murmured "πr^2".

My legs to jelly they reduce
Each time they breathe "hypotenuse"
And nearly drive me to distraction
When they chide a vulgar fraction.
Will you shun this love of mine,
When shape and symmetry divine
Most shameless thoughts in me arouse
Of perfect cones - beneath a blouse?

Let's be together, you and I
And (dare I say it) multiply.

Come share my home, come share my
    bath
And wallow in the aftermath!

The COMPLETE WIT & WHIMSEY

In about 1998 I entered a poetry competition at a literary festival. Because the occasion was a "festival", the theme of the competition was "festivals and holidays" interpreted pretty broadly. When I did a bit of research on the subject, I was amazed at just how many public holidays other countries award themselves. And not only the number of holidays, but the reasons behind them. Well. we're not like that! We're British, and when we want to celebrate, we jolly well do it our way!

THE BRITISH STYLE

When festivals and holidays
Assail our sceptred isle,
We stay sedate and celebrate
In sober British style:
In other lands they march to bands
And laugh and shout like cranks,
But we applaud (though slightly bored)
- The closing of the banks.

When May Day dawns on Moscow's lawns
Oh, what an awesome sight:
For there displayed all on parade
Comes Mother Russia's might.
From pride or fear the people cheer
And streets are lined with tanks,
While Britain quietly celebrates
The closing of the banks.

In mid-July in old Versailles
Bastille Day comes along.
The French don't work, but go beserk
And sing their national song.
They drink all day their Beaujolais
And throw around their francs,
But Britain quietly celebrates
The closing of the banks.

On Mothers' Day in San José
The greatest and the least,
By making love in hills above,
Perpetuate the feast.
They kiss and hug on pampas rug,
Entwining arms and flanks,
But Britain quietly celebrates
The closing of the banks.

Some countries say Armed Forces' Day
Is greater than the rest.
In every town the soldiers clown,
All dressed up in their best.
They deem it fun to wave a gun
And fire a hundred blanks.
But Britain quietly celebrates
The closing of the banks.

From south to north July the fourth
Engulfs the USA:
In parts of Maine they go insane
And dance the night away.
It's rather frantic Trans-Atlantic,
Leave it to the Yanks.
We'll celebrate with dignity
The closing of the banks.

In Chester, Leicester, Cirencester,
Folk get out of breath
Doing rounds of schools and grounds
At fêtes far worse than death.
The rain pours down, we almost drown,
The deluge warps the planks,
And soggy sandwiches proclaim
The closing of the banks.

Part 2: IN LIGHTEST VEIN

The religious divide in Ireland was very much in the forefront of the news when I wrote this poem in the mid-1990's. The poem is called "Paddy's Car".

PADDY'S CAR

Paddy took his old car for a service:
The engine, it stank to high hell.
The mechanic said "Paddy, I'm nervous,
This car's got a terrible smell.

Now, we're living in times of inflation,
So I'll just do the work that I'm forced,
But you'll poison the whole population
If I don't fit another exhaust.

And to stop your conviction for murder
There's one other thing I can do;
I've a good catalytic converter
I can fit for a fiver or two."

Then Paddy sat down on a girder.
"Now listen young fellow," he said,
"I'll have no Catalytic converter.
Fit the Protestant model instead!"

Now here's a very short poem about a chap called Bert. He's a well-known local character and he's always got some tale of woe. When I saw him the other day, his latest grumble was about what happened last week when he cut himself shaving. This little poem is called "Bert's Lament".

BERT'S LAMENT

I cut myself while shaving,
A rather nasty nip.
A great big crimson blob appeared
Upon my lower lip.

I blotted and I dabbed it,
I rinsed it in the sink,
But when I ate my breakfast,
My Shredded Wheat turned pink.

Now cuts like that don't heal well,
They always take a while.
You've got to keep your lips pursed
And never ever smile.

I walked into the village
To buy some milk and bread,
When someone said "Good morning, Bert"
I'd grunt and nod my head.

But when I saw the Vicar's wife,
I gave my widest grin,
And when I said "Hello, my dear"
The blood ran down my chin.

The COMPLETE WIT & WHIMSEY

We have to be very careful what we say these days. We're living in times of political correctness. But all countries have their pet caricatures of other countries, and more often than not these caricatures are actually founded in affection, not hatred. We learn them as children, and no doubt have already passed them on to the next generation. Here's a little poem along these lines.

WORLD TOUR

When I was at my Daddy's knee
He kissed me once and he said to me
"Love thy neighbours, love them do,
Even if they're not like you."
So I love black folks, white folks, Asians,
I love folks from all the nations.
I'm glad I have no prejudice
- Except for thoughts that go like this:

The Scots

Scotsmen wear the kilt and sporran,
Speak a tongue entirely foreign.
They're very hairy, big and strong,
And play the bagpipes all night long.
They'll drink a dram or two, and then
They'll hunt for haggis in the glen.
And one of life's most deadly dangers
Is watching Celtic versus Rangers!

The Welsh

The Welsh distrust their English
    neighbour,
Dig for coal, and vote for Labour.
They're all called Williams, Jones and
    Powell
And live in towns without a vowel
(Not simple names like Bath and
    Bedford).
Some get drunk at the Eisteddfod,
Others at a Rugby fling,
And even when they talk, they sing.

The Irish

The Irish always want a fight,
They're not sure why, but know they're
    right.
From County Antrim down to Kerry
People drink and get quite merry,
Go to church and know what sin is -
Drinking someone else's Guinness.
In Saint Patrick is their hope
Because he's Catholic, like the Pope.

The Americans

Americans seem loud and brash,
And always have a lot of cash.
They all speak English rather funny
And call their wives and sweethearts
    'honey'
A tramp's a bum, a pub's a bar,
The pavement's where they drive a car,
And when a young man looks his best
He's in suspenders and a vest!

The French

Many things about the French
Make the Anglo-Saxon blench:
They eat dead snails, they eat dead frogs,
For all I know, they eat dead dogs.
French girls are wicked, we believe,
Wear French knickers, take French
    leave.
Perhaps a small increase in fun'll
Come now there's a Channel Tunnel.

Part 2: IN LIGHTEST VEIN

The Germans
Germans eat sauerkraut and wurst
And have a most enormous thirst.
Because of this they grow quite large
And always want to be in charge.
Be careful in the Fatherland,
For very many things are banned,
And those that aren't you'll quickly see
Are more or less compulsory!

The Italians
Italians used to lead the way
In culture. Now they've gone astray.
They used to paint and sculpt and sing,
Now don't do much of anything
Except encourage maids to yield
Or kick a ball around a field,
Where have you gone, you lovely
    Borgias?
Cesare bold, Lucrezia gorgeous.

The Spanish
Spanish girls have fiery eyes.
They like to dance and show their thighs,
And if you know one well, she lets
You practice on her castanets.
Spanish men uphold machismo:
They grab a nasty pointed gismo,
Then off they go and seek a bull
And do things quite unspeakable.

The Russians
The Russian is a vodka drinker,
Loves Prokoviev and Glinka,
And now he's ditched that Marxist crap,
He's really quite a decent chap.
So, after all those Commie lies,
Perhaps it's time to fraternise:
"Hello Darren, my name's Tanya,
Sorry Sharon, do-svidaniya."

The Arabs
Arabs make much use of camels:
First they ride, then eat, these mammals.
Some of them remain quite tribal,
- Still wear clothes like in the Bible.
Arabs used to live in tents,
Some for ladies, some for gents,
But now they're rich, for 'neath their soil
They dug a hole and found some oil.

The Japanese
The Japanese are very rich
And most of them conceive an itch
Around the world in groups to wander
In a coach or in a Honda.
It really can't be very nice
To eat raw fish on beds of rice;
But some of them grow very plump
And wrestle with each other's rump.

And finally .
But what about us English folk:
Do others think we're just a joke?
What's the image we convey
To those who pass along our way?
Well, truth to tell, I'm glad to shrink
From guessing what the others think
Because they're not like you and me:
They're ... well, they're foreigners, you
    see!

The COMPLETE WIT & WHIMSEY

A few years ago, whenever weather forecasters were discussed, for some reason one person's name would nearly always spring to mind before all others. I wonder why! We loved him really, but after the famous hurricane of 1987 were we sure he could get his weather information right? Were we sure he could get anything right? Even at home? Anyway, although this little poem dedicated to him was written sometime in the 1990's and is therefore somewhat dated, his name must be preserved for future generations. This poem is, of course, called "Fish out of Water".

FISH OUT OF WATER

A whirlwind take you, Michael Fish:
That is now my greatest wish.
Acting on advice from you
My family planned a barbecue
They came from Surrey, Kent and Cheshire
Expecting sunshine and high pressure.
Instead, it bucketed with rain.
I think we've reason to complain.
Why do you always get things wrong?
(And it's been going on so long!)
Your tendency to err - does this
Intrude upon domestic bliss?
Perhaps your teeth derive their gleam
Through cleaning them with shaving cream?
Perhaps you microwave the cat
Or sweep the lawn and mow the mat,
Or shower beneath the garden hose
Or dress in someone else's clothes,
Or take the goldfish for a walk,
Eat Shredded Wheat with knife and fork?
Does Mrs Fish say "Michael dear,
You're putting toast inside your ear."

Our soggy, boggy barbecue
Was due exclusively to you.
So that is now my greatest wish:
A whirlwind take you Michael Fish.

Part 2: IN LIGHTEST VEIN

There's a man called Harry Graham who wrote a series of hilarious, though somewhat sadistic, verses called the Bab Ballads (or is it Bad Ballads?). He gave me the idea for these verses. One of Harry's best known ballads goes like this:

"Billy, in one of his nice new sashes,
Fell in the fire and was burned to ashes.
Now, although the room grows chilly,
We haven't the heart to poke poor Billy".

UNKIND CUTS

Aunt Ethel, on the Tour Eiffel,
Leant too far over, down she fell.
Said Uncle Walter, ever thrifty,
"What a waste of twelve francs, fifty!"

Little Arthur, with a gun,
Blew his Dad to Kingdom Come.
"Oh" said Mother, "That was cruel.
But hurry, you'll be late for school."

"Private Jones" the Sergeant roared,
"Fifteen shots, and nothing scored!
You stupid imbecile!" yelled he,
"No, please don't point that gun at ."

"Lucy darling" said her mother
"Please don't tease your baby brother.
Nappies go on babies' rears,
Not tightly wrapped round mouth and ears."

Ricardo - what a craftsman, he:
Weaving things of quality.
And there's nothing he can't do with raffia,
Interviewing for the Mafia.

Said mother "Come and say hello to Vicar."
Sweet Elsie lisped "Please Vicar, tell me how
It is you do not look remotely bovine,
Yet mother says you're married to a cow."

On holiday in Cairo, Joe
Thought he'd like another week,
So, being somewhat short of dough,
He offered missus to a sheikh.
But one thing Joseph didn't know:
'Twas gentlemen the sheikh preferred,
And so the missus sold him Joe
And ran off with a randy Kurd.

The COMPLETE WIT & WHIMSEY

Here is a poem from my first book, which some readers were kind enough to say was their favourite. There's a small group of words in English that seem to hang together and, for me, conjure up little furry Hobbit-like creatures with the odd monster thrown in. This little fantasy was great fun to write.

DANGER AFOOT

A furry brown creature popped out of his hole.
He wasn't a mouse and he wasn't a mole.
Another small creature was passing his way,
So the furry one cheerily called out "Good day",
Then he said as he busily scratched in the dirt
"As you plainly can see, I'm a Lert."

The other ignored him and went on his way,
So the Lert darted after him, calling "I say,
Don't you know that it's rude not to give a reply?
If you choose to eschew me, I'd like to know why."
So the other one said "Well, to tell you the truth
(As if you can't guess) I'm a Loof.

But since you're out walking, I'll walk with you, too.
We might find some custard, or rhubarb to chew."
So the Lert and the Loof wandered into a wood
Where, in front of an oak tree, an animal stood.
He was juggling three skittles, two balls and a quoit.
"Why, hello there" he said, "I'm a Droit."

"Do you mind if I join you, I'm bored all alone."
And the others said "Fine. It's no fun on your own."
Then behind them another voice said "Well, I never!
A Lert and a Loof and a Droit out together."
They turned and beheld a smart beast in a suit
Who said "By the way, I'm a Stute."

"Come join us" they said. He replied "Well, I could."
So the four friends walked deeper into the dark wood.
Then the Stute and the Droit and the Loof and the Lert
Encountered a beast in a corduroy shirt
Who said "Please don't walk here, folks, you'll never get past.
If you really must know, I'm a Ghast!"

Part 2: IN LIGHTEST VEIN

"What's wrong?" asked the Lert and the Droit and the Stute.
And the Ghast said "You're close to the lair of a brute."
Then a huge fearsome animal rushed out of the gloom
And roared "Poor little creatures, prepare for your doom!
Prepare to consign your poor souls into Limbo.
With my paws on my hips, I'm a Kimbo!"

Then the Kimbo rushed after the creatures all five,
"Ho! Ho!" shouted he, "Lerts? I eat them alive.
As for Loofs, Droits and Stutes, why I soak them in oil,
Put them into a pan, slowly bring to the boil,
Then simmer till tender and squeeze in a lime,
And garnish with parsley and thyme."

Then he suddenly staggered and blundered around,
And the forest floor shook as he fell to the ground.
Then they saw their deliverer, handsome and broad
And strong and courageous, who flourished a sword;
And he murmured, as onto a boulder he leapt,
"As you doubtless can see, I'm a Dept.

Now take my advice and go back whence you came.
More Kimbos live here, and they're all just the same."
So they thanked the brave Dept and jumped head over heels,
And raced back to safety with rapturous squeals:
The Lert and the Droit and the Stute and the Ghast
And the Loof - yes, of course, he was last.

They came out of the wood as the sun went to bed.
They were hungry and tired, but so glad they weren't dead.
Then they saw just ahead, as the light turned to mauve,
A large custard lake and a sweet rhubarb grove.
So they all ate their fill, and they drank the lake dry
While, smiling, the moon rode the sky.

The COMPLETE WIT & WHIMSEY

Here's another little story where the words come out to play.

JUST THE JOB

Poor Jim sat dishevelled, his head on his knee,
Distracted, distraught and disgruntled was he.
For seven long months he had searched for a job,
But nobody wanted him. Then with a sob
He cried "All they can do is disdain and disparage -
And where there's no work there's no marriage."

For his sweetheart had told him "I'm sorry, my dear,
You're unkempt, you've no job, so you've had it, I fear."
And so she discarded him, went her own way
And began seeing more of a sales rep from Cray.
He thought "Never again will I see darling Joan"
And he gave a disconsolate groan.

It wasn't as if he'd not tried to find work.
He wasn't an idler, he wasn't a jerk.
He'd applied for translation jobs- did he know Greek?
Or Chinese or Arabic, what did he speak?
Well, what about Russian? - he left feeling frantic:
His degree was in Ancient Icelandic.

He wrote to a Bishop who needed a clerk,
He was seventy-nine and was losing his spark,
But the interview over, the Bishop, said he,
"I note you're a Papist, well, I'm C of E.
Though I'm old and I'm frail and I'm riddled with rheumatism
There's a limit I place on ecumenism!"

Then slowly down-market Jim went after work,
In industrial Lancashire groped through the mirk.
An assembly-line job he thought he had landed
Till the foreman explained all machines were right-handed.
Then he knew right away he would be of no worth:
He'd been (sadly) left-handed from birth.

Part 2: IN LIGHTEST VEIN

His hobbies were birds (yes, he loved ornithology)
And crosswords and things (he adored etymology),
So applied, as he thought, to update C.O.D.
But they told him the advert was not error-free:
They'd not spelt 'entomologist' quite like they ought,
So he wasn't the bugger they sought.

That's why Jim sat there sighing, his head on his knee,
Distracted, distraught and disconsolate, he.
Meanwhile, in Whitehall, in a basement quite sinistery
A debate was in progress, involving the Ministry
Of Espionage (also known as Min Spies) -
Quite a few had turned up in disguise.

The Chairman said "Well, we agree the essentials,
But where will we find such a mix of credentials
For this specialised work? There's just no-one, I fear
Even at eighty-five thousand a year.
But we'll advertise daily, just let the thing run,
The broadsheets, of course, and the Sun."

Next morning young Jim, who was still feeling sad,
Read with amazement a vacancy ad:
'Left-handed Catholic, an expert on birds,
Must be *au fait* with unusual words,
Some knowledge required of Ancient Icelandic
For a salary ...' (this was gigantic!)

Jim applied for the job and was greatly acclaimed,
No-one disparaged him, no-one disdained:
He was dained, he was paraged, so, humming a tune,
He quickly 'phoned Joan (he was over the moon.)
"I'm about to get married" she said "Down in Cray.
I'm sorry, Jim. Have a nice day."

"Do I cave in?" thought Jim, "Oh dear, what do I do?"
Then he made up his mind and to Reykjavik flew,
Where he met his assistant, a ravishing blonde,
A left-handed Catholic, a female James Bond,
An expert in words, and a skilful bird-spotter.
He adored his young Greta Svensdottir.

The COMPLETE WIT & WHIMSEY

No longer distraught or disconsolate, he,
Distracted, disgruntled, or head on his knee.
Now he's consolate, tracted, and gruntled and traught
And proud to have won the long battle he'd fought.
He's improved his appearance, he's hevelled and kempt
And in love at the second attempt!

Part 2: IN LIGHTEST VEIN

This little bit of onomatopoeia may induce nostalgia for the steam age.

GIRL'S THOUGHTS FROM A TRAIN

Shhhh, shhhhh, shhhhh, shhhhh,
Shhhh, shhhhh, shhhhh, shhhhh,
Shhhh, shhhh, shhhh, shhhh,
Shhhh, shhhh, shhhh, shhhh...

Fiddle-dee-dah, fiddle-dee-dee
I'm going to Hull to see Billy McGee,
Billy McGee, Billy McGee,
Lemonade, lollipops, Billy and me.
Billy McGee, Billy McGee,
When I see him I'll kiss him and kiss him and
Kiss him and kiss him and kiss him and kiss him
And hullaballoo, hullaballah,
Billy is silly for living so far.
Billy McGee, Billy McGee,
Sunshine and bicycles, Billy and me.
Billy McGee, Billy McGee,
When I see him we'll cuddle and cuddle and
Cuddle and cuddle and cuddle and cuddle
And kalamazee, kalamazoo,
I'm Little Bo-Peep, he's Little Boy Blue.
Billy McGee, Billy McGee,
Strawberries and teddy bears, Billy and me.
Billy McGee, Billy McGee,
When I see him I'll giggle and giggle and
Giggle and giggle and giggle and giggle
With glee.
Billy and me.

Hull is not dull, it's got Billy McGee!

Shhhhhhhhhhhhhhhhhhhhh!

The COMPLETE WIT & WHIMSEY

On a recent holiday in Cornwall, I found that the National Trust seems to have gained control of much of the county without a shot being fired. Even where there is no National Trust property, they run well-signed car parks for strangers unaware that Council-controlled street parking is available at a fraction of the cost. There seems to be a parallel here to a practice popular in Cornwall a few generations ago.

READY WRECKONER

In days of old, so we are told,
The talk in Cornish docks
Was of the light at dead of night
That sprang up on the rocks.

*

The light appeared when tempest neared
To lure unknowing strangers -
A cargo boat would shoreward float,
Unconscious of the dangers.

*

Aye, ships would blunder, men would plunder
'Twas their livelihood.
By dark deceit they gained their meat
And all the spoils they could.

*

This practice still provokes a thrill,
But now it's done by day:
The National Trust decrees you must
Large sums of money pay.

*

They lure each car with signs bizarre
Away from modest fees,
For Cornwall County's now their bounty:
What a jolly wheeze!

*

Oh, National Trust (get-rich-or-bust)
Your message is quite clear:
Full fathom five in pocket dive
And pay the cash, m'dear.

Part 2: IN LIGHTEST VEIN

There is one particular work of art that has been shrouded in mystery ever since it was created in Italy in the year 1500. You know the one I mean. Well, puzzle no more. I've sussed out the mystery of that smile and can now reveal all. So come with me to that studio in Italy more than 500 years ago, and let us eavesdrop on what really happened.

THAT PAINTING: AT LAST THE TRUTH

"You sitta here" the artist said.
The sitter shook her noble head.
"I wanna sitta over there,
You gonna have to move da chair."
The artist sighed his acquiescence
(Why ladies always act like peasants?)
He said "And why you hide you hair?
You head, I told you, must be bare.
But no, you wearing da mantilla
Surrounded with da lacy frilla.
How can I paint you lovely tresses?
And you, what gotta lotsa dresses,
Green and blue and pink and red,
You wear a black-a one instead.
Go home, Signora, change you gear
And when you done it, come back here."

The lady rose up from her seat
And tossed her head and stamped her feet.
"I pay you money, yet you dare
To tell-a me what things to wear.
I don't-a need-a you permission.
I please myself - or no commission!
There plenty painters, plenty men-a
In Firenze and Sienna
Who paint me cheap-a, not so dear-a,
Help me save-a lotsa lire."

Sensing his defeat was nigh,
The artist summoned one more try.
"OK Signora, I agree
If you will leave the choice to me
Of background. What I have in mind:
The town-a stand, the river wind

Down from the hills, where trees-a grow
Neat and tidy in a row.
For this-a scene give you complaisance -
It's typical of the Renaissance."

But no. She signified dissent
And said "I will-a not relent.
I just want rocks, all big, no small
And do some water. That's-a all."
He saw the triumph in her eye
As he consented to comply.

Conscious that he'd been defeated,
The lady's portrait he completed
With her wish in strict compliance.
But yet, some gesture of defiance
He was not able to resist -
A symbol that would not be missed:

Her smile would show the world, thought he
Her arrogance in victory,
The triumph playing round her lips,
The hand that held the winning chips.

She must have sensed his little game,
For when she saw it in its frame
To buy the portrait she demurred
And walked away without a word.

They spoke of it from Rome to Pisa:
Da Vinci snubbed by Mona Lisa!

We all like a quiet moment to be alone with our thoughts.

THOUGHTS

I like to sit and reminisce,
To reminisce on that and thisce,
The girls with whom I've shared a kisce,
My lovely wife, our married blisce.
So, I repeat, with emphasisce,
Without the slightest prejudisce,
A pleasure that I'd hate to misce
Is just to sit and reminisce.

Little girls will one day be assertive teenagers and assertive mothers. Then watch out, fellows. Meanwhile, they practise on defenceless Grandpas.

THE PHEASANT SHOOT

She said "They're shooting birds again
All over Stancombe Hill,
Those men in waxy coats who have
That yucky urge to kill."

I spoke of long tradition
In the British countryside
But spoke without conviction
And without a sense of pride.

She looked at me impatiently,
And ten-year-old's contempt.
"They breed them just to kill them!"
I made one last attempt.

"Perhaps they eat the crops up
Or attack the likes of us.
They can be rather viscious
So we have to make a fuss!"

She looked at me pathetically
And told me right away:
"It can't be very pleasant
Being savaged by a pheasant!"
Then she tossed her head
    And flounced outside to play.

Part 2: IN LIGHTEST VEIN

Watch out! There's a rather strange creature roaming around Africa at the moment. This is the story of where he came from.

THE RHINOPOTPHANTEBEEST

Near the hot Kalahari
Where night skies are starry,
A rather strange creature sat under the shade.
He was sad, he was lonely,
For he was the only
Rhinopotphantebeest God ever made.

His mother explained:
Once it rained and it rained,
And a rhino and hippo had strayed from their herd.
In the floods they had tarried,
Got lonely, so married,
And brought a girl Rhinopot into the world.

An elephant, too
Got cut off, and did woo
A lovely young wildebeest left on her own.
She gave birth to a son,
And in years filled with fun
A strapping young Phantebeest slowly had grown.

Yes, the Phantebeest grew
And the Rhinopot, too
Until one day they found out why everyone jeered:
They had no-one to date with
And no-one to mate with,
For no-one quite like them had ever appeared.

Then came the wet season
And, for the same reason
They both slipped away, and 'twas then that they met:
Two creatures rejected
They quickly elected
To marry, to live, and to love and forget.

And that's how, months later,
To mater and pater
The Rhinopotphantebeest came to be born,
Unique of his kind.
And that's why we find
Him sitting and brooding, alone and forlorn.

But what he didn't know
Was that ages ago
The rains had caused other strange unions to bloom,
And a creature so tender
Of feminine gender
That evening came tip-toeing out of the gloom.

And, as she approached him,
She softly reproached him,
Said "Why's a fine fellow like you looking blue?"
He cried "Pray, who are you?"
She said "Don't you know who?
I'm a Phantepotrhinobeest, nearly like you!"

What bliss and what joy
For this girl and this boy.
They kissed and they cuddled and vowed to be true.
"I'm content with my lot"
He said "Though you are not
A Rhinopotphantebeest, darling, you'll do!"

Part 2: IN LIGHTEST VEIN

Yes, it's really become necessary to issue a Government health warning on foreign holidays. Before you venture overseas, you are strongly advised to read the words that follow!

ADVICE TO TRAVELLERS ABROAD

When you're in a foreign land
Be sure their ways you understand.
Never drink the local water
And do not kiss a native's daughter.
Never stroke the animals
And do not speak to cannibals
(They'll cut you into little bits
And serve you up with peas and chips.)
Be careful where you have a swim -
Untreated sewage can be grim:
(Don't try the crawl in certain oceans
You'll just be going through the motions.
Don't wade or paddle in strange pools,
You'll find you fall between two stools).
At night-time in the USA
Never from your hotel stray.
Remember- few things can be horrider
Than being mugged by thugs in Florida
(And though by day it might be sunny,
Americans talk English funny.)
You may get tanned a lovely bronze,
But do weigh up the pros and cons:

If all you want is sea and sand,
Food in belly, beer in hand,
You're better off on Blackpool's beaches

Or (marginally) Bognor Regis.

The COMPLETE WIT & WHIMSEY

THEME AND VARIATIONS
The limerick about the lady from Riga and the tiger has been doing the rounds for generations - certainly since the 1940's when I first heard it. In those days, of course, Riga, as pronounced by the English-speaking world, rhymed with tiger, whereas now it is universally pronounced 'Reega,' thus rendering the original limerick unworkable. This is a pity. Perhaps the time has come to suggest a few variations on the theme!

THEME:

There was a young lady from Riga,
Who smiled as she rode on a tiger.
They returned from the ride
With the lady inside
And the smile on the face of the tiger.

VARIATIONS:

There was a young lady called Rita,
Who smiled as she rode on a cheetah.
The cause of her smiles
Was that every 10 miles
He only consumed half a litre.

There was a young fellow named Brian,
Who smiled as he rode on a lion.
He said "You think I'm frivolous,
'Cause these things are carnivorous,
But this one's a toothless and shy 'un."

A lady who lived near the Sphinx,
Smiled as she rode on a lynx,
But admitted "Indeed,
He's a pretty poor steed,
For he's lame, he has fleas and he stinx!"

There once was an erudite shepherd,
Who smiled as he rode on a leopard.
He said "It's incredible,
They're really quite edible,
Roasted, and salted and peppered."

A grandma from north Nicaragua
Smiled as she rode on a jaguar.
When she shot the beast dead,
RSPCA said
"Goodness me, what a bloodthirsty hag you are!"

There was an expatriate Tamil,
Who winced as he rode on a camel.
Apart from the heat
He put up with a seat
That some Arabs had made from enamel.

Part 2: IN LIGHTEST VEIN

When a BBC chap came to interview me upon the publication of my second book, he arrived at a time when a very large fungus had taken root in the front garden. It was well over a foot tall already. Goodness knows where it came from. Anyway, the BBC fellow challenged me to write a few lines about it, and this bit of doggerel was the result.

FAME AT LAST

In my garden, unannounced,
Up through the soil had leapt
A mushroom white, at dead of night
While everybody slept.

It grew and grew, and by Day Two
It stood four feet in height,
And by Day Three 'twas like a tree
And blotted out the light.

By now a chap called Humphrys
From the BBC had rung us
To ask if he could come and see
And interview this fungus.

The national press turned up in force
The headlines were exciting:
"Winchcombe Poet's Huge Success"
And "Not Mushroom For Writing."

Then people came from miles around:
The first ones came at dawn.
They brought their brood and lots of food
And camped upon the lawn.

The famous even came along
To marvel and to stare.
Dennis Skinner brought his dinner
So did Tony Blair.

They spoke of it in Parliament,
Discussed it in the Knesset,
And when it grew to ten feet, two
The Pope popped round to bless it.

Now botanists respect me
And say they all think well of me.
I've had the greatest accolade -
A kiss from David Bellamy.

And now the mushroom's gone. It died
As quickly as it came.
To my disgust it bit the dust -
How transient is fame!

But I'm quite philosophical:
Things could have been much worse.
At least I know where I can go -
Indoors, to write this verse!

The COMPLETE WIT & WHIMSEY

Now, do we all know what a "twitcher" is? Yes, that's right. A "twitcher" is an anorak who does bird-watching. There are some parts of the country that attract rare birds, - Norfolk and the Scilly Isles, for example, where long-distance migrants often pause for a rest. Well, this poem's about a very young twitcher – a lad of eight called Gerald, who has prevailed upon his Dad to take him bird-watching. But Dad, who has little interest in the subject, forgot to pack one vital item – The Readers' Digest Book of Birds. So, here's a little poem entitled "Sort of ....a Bird".

SORT OF ... A BIRD

To northern parts of Norfolk
The father took the child,
Where birds galore invade the shore –
A region bleak and wild.

*

Now little Gerald, barely eight,
Had plans to join the twitchers.
But Dad forgot his bird-book –
That one with all the pictures.

*

And here stands Gerald, keen to start
In olive anorak,
While poor old Dad is looking sad
In wellies and a mac.

*

They make their way along the shore,
Binoculars in hand,
And soon the lad starts poking Dad
And points towards the sand.

*

"Daddy, what's that big bird there,
That's standing all alone:
The one that's smashing sort of snails
Upon that sort of stone?"

*

"Er ...it's an oyster-catcher, Gerald,
At least that's what I think:
It's sort of black and white, son,
And its beak is sort of pink."

*

"Look, Daddy, there's another bird,
It's sitting on the sea
And sort of catching sort of fish.
Oh, what can that one be?"

*

Er ....it's an oyster-catcher, Gerald,
You can tell it by its wings:
They're sort of black around the back
With sort of - fluffy things.

*

"Daddy, there's another bird,
It's coming in to land.
And now it's got its sort of beak
All sticking in the sand."

*

"Er.....it's an oyster-catcher, Gerald,
You can tell it by its legs:
They nest in sort of hollows
And lay brownish sort of eggs."

*

"Well, Daddy, what's that one up there
That's flying very high?
And now it's sort of pointing down
And diving from the sky."

*

Er ......it's an oyster-catcher, Gerald,
You can tell it by its head;
It's sort of green and purple
With a little bit of red."

Part 2: IN LIGHTEST VEIN

"Daddy, Daddy, look down there,
There's one that's sort of bald.
It's sort of eating sort of mud.
Oh. Daddy, what's it called?"

"It's an oyster-catcher, Gerald,
Its beak is sharp and curved.
I hope it hasn't seen us,
'Cause it hates to be observed.

*

It's a vicious little bugger,
You should see it when it's mad,
And it feeds on silly little boys
Who irritate their Dad!"

One of my daughters (Sue or Helen, I'm not sure which), who was expecting her baby to arrive in about three weeks, told me at the time that she felt like a big, fat slug. That reminded me that when I was in the garden one day, I heard a funny noise coming from the direction of the compost heap, and there to my astonishment I saw this slug with a big smile on his face singing a little song. It wasn't very musical: it was all on one note, but it was certainly a happy song. So I wrote it down, and here it is.

SONG OF THE HAPPY SLUG

Sluggy, sluggy, uggy-wuggy,
Soggy-woggy, squish.
Cabby-wabbage, beany-weeny,
Chewy-woo, I wish!
Biggy-wiggy gobble-wobble,
Slimey-wimey, squelch.
Fatty-watty tummy-wummy,
Indigesty belch.

Girly-wurly sluggy-wuggy,
Soggy-woggy woo.
Sloshy-woshy kissy-wissy,
Sluggy say 'I do'.
Girly-wurly preggy-weggy,
Fatty-watty tum:
Chubby little teeny-weenies,
Sluggy Dad and Mum.

The COMPLETE WIT & WHIMSEY

For the romantics among us, here is a love poem straight from the heart. What young lady would not like to hear these words on 14th February?

MY VALENTINE

My love - you're like an unmade bed,
You look a proper mess.
You've got your jumper inside out
And ketchup down your dress.

You wear those tatty flip-flops
And lollop round the floor.
You chuck the breakfast tea-leaves
Outside the kitchen door.

Your hair looks like a nest of snakes:
To comb it you've forgotten.
You've got a ladder in your tights
- And I love you something rotten!

SNOW WHITE AND THE SEVEN LONELY DWARVES

Snow White, we think, was quite content:
She had a home and paid no rent.
But though her life seemed utter bliss,
There was another side to this:
She had to strive by night and day
To keep those naughty dwarves at bay.
Some were easy, some were not,
Let's think about this little lot:

Bashful posed no threat at all,
He might approach her, then he'd stall.
One quick peck, then crimson red
He'd hastily retire to bed.

Sleepy clearly found her boring -
One quick hug, then he'd be snoring.

Sneezy, proposition uttered,
Usually just coughed and spluttered,
But sometimes said things quite obscene,
Secure with anti-histamine.

Part 2: IN LIGHTEST VEIN

Dopey, when he'd had his fix
Tried the most alarming tricks,
But never wished to consummate,
He'd rather just hallucinate.

Grumpy was a silly dolt,
He spent the whole time finding fault,

And Happy - well, it even niggled -
All he did was sat and giggled.

Doc she viewed with consternation:
Nostalgic for his first vocation
He begged her let him remedy
His skills at gynaecology -
An offer she, of course, declined
And told him he'd a dirty mind.

And so, despite their antics, she
Somehow preserved her chastity.

But then one evening someone knocked
Upon the door, the dwarves all flocked
To meet the caller. There he stood,
A handsome man in cloak and hood.
"Hello dwarves, remember me?
I'd like to stay a while" said he.
The dwarves could not believe their eyes
And said "Well, what a great surprise!
Please come on in and have a brandy.
Snow White, meet our cousin Randy."

The COMPLETE WIT & WHIMSEY

I suppose students still swot like mad for their 'O' and 'A' Levels as we used to do? Swotting was very much part of the culture of the 1940's and 1950's when I was at Grammar School. But then, there was no TV to watch or play-stations to divert us. Even pop music hadn't been invented. Nor had teenagers. I remember passing most evenings either doing homework or swotting for exams, and getting very tired doing it, as the student in this little poem does.

REVISION

See the student in his teens
Come to quite a late decision,
Lying on his bed in jeans
Sees the merit of revision.

Seizes textbooks, wildly crams,
For Monday brings the tricky bit:
His three most difficult exams -
Science, Maths and English Lit.

One hour later learnéd tracts
Are thrust aside. He shuts his eyes,
Reciting to himself the facts
That buzz around his brain like flies:

I wandered lonely as a cloud,
Now, what's that bit on acid rain?
And all at once I saw a crowd
With global warming on the brain.

The curfew tolls the knell of day
And gas comes under whatsit's Law.
The ploughman homeward plods his way
And slips in H_2SO_4.

This afternoon it's England-Wales,
And Wales look quite invincible.
I must do Canterbury Tales,
And what's that Greek bloke's Principle?

Pollution is a nasty thing
Environmentally bad news.
Is Thane a sort of Scottish king
Or part of the hypotenuse?

The Ancient Mariner is mad,
As well as being very old:
He must have looked a bit like Dad.
Does cryogenics deal with cold?

The curfew tolls the lonely cloud
As England win the mauls and rucks.
There's Chaucer waving to the crowds.
Pollution comes from cars and trucks.

What good it trigonometry?
They'll have to play like men inspired.
At least I know some geometry.
I wish I didn't feel so tired.

The car fumes toll for Nell and Dai,
The Welsh are plodding up the hills.
And who's this sailor passing by
And pinching all their daffodils?

His father comes to call the lad.
"Forget your homework for a while,
The game's just started" says his Dad.
The student smiles a secret smile.

Part 2: IN LIGHTEST VEIN

For some of us, those last few months or years might mean becoming institutionalised, and perhaps losing our identity. This must be irritating, especially for those who were once well-known stage or screen performers. Here's a lament from one of them.

THE FINAL CURTAIN

Forgive me if I sound downcast
And shed a little tear,
I'm in a nursing home at last
And known to all as 'dear'.

I'm now too old to tread those boards
I trod for many a year,
I miss the plaudits of the hordes
For now I'm just plain 'dear'.

I used to be a household name,
My fame spread far and near,
But now, alas, what good is fame:
I'm simply known as 'dear'.

They flocked in thousands just to see
My Hamlet or my Lear,
The public thought the world of me
But now I'm simply 'dear'.

So stick a tube right up my nose,
Another in my ear,
Or amputate my little toes
But – please don't call me 'dear'.

Poke and prod below my waist
And gaze inside my rear,
Deprive me of my sense of taste
But – please don't call me 'dear'.

I'll let you all administer
Those jabs you know I fear
And do things cruel and sinister
But – please don't call me 'dear'.

Oh, here I lie, and soon I'll die,
I feel the end draw near,
But then at least if death is nigh
- It puts an end to 'dear'.

Here's a bit of pure nonsense for cat lovers

PEDRO THE PUSSY-CAT

Now Pedro was a **pussy-cat,**
Who lived in sunny Spain,
A **cat** from **Catalonia,**
His home was down a drain.

The drain led to the **catacombs**
Where he would roam around,
Until he reached a river wide
That flowed beneath the ground.

And there he'd **catch** the fish he loved
That swam beneath the street,
He killed them with a **catapult,**
Then had ice-cream for sweet.

He kept a daily **catalogue**
Of all the fish he caught,
And **catfish** was the one he loved,
The one he always sought.

Yes, **catfish** was the one for him,
His really favourite sort,
The **category** he loved best,
They filled each waking thought.

But then came Pedro's sad demise,
With health he was not blest.
He'd **cataracts** in both his eyes,
Catarrh upon his chest.

Then came a **catastrophic** blow,
A **catatonic** fit,
And, sadly. Pedro breathed his last,
This mortal coil he quit.

His **catafalque** stood in the church,
A **caterpillar** green,
The likes of Pedro, folks agreed,
Will never more be seen.

Part 2: IN LIGHTEST VEIN

These are just what they say they are – revised versions of a few nursery rhymes and related bits.

NURSERY RHYMES etc. (revised)

Mother Hubbard, in tears, shook her head
"There's no food for you, Fido" she said.
And the dog, with loud groans
Thought "Two weeks without bones!"
So he ate Mother Hubbard instead.

Boy Blue oft neglected his sheep.
He claimed he was always asleep.
There's no truth to that yarn:
He'd be down at the barn
Making hay with his girl-friend Bo-Peep.

Convinced he was well out of sight,
Jack Horner gave t'pie a great bite.
Then he stuck in his thumb
And got thumped by his Mum
Yelling "Why can't you eat the thing right?,"

Willie Winkie in nightshirt (no drawers),
Breaks all of the decency laws.
He'll caper about
'Twixt the houses and shout
Obscenities through the front doors.

Georgie Porgie, with lecherous leers,
Reduced all the maidens to tears.
His sexual harassment
Caused them embarrassment
Till the Judge gave him 25 years.

As Miss Muffet sat eating her porridge
A spider came, feeling for forage.
When it tickled her ass
She leapt up from the grass
And kept running until she reached
    Norwich.

On the wall Humpty Dumpty did say
"Why should I not sit up here, pray?"
Then the masonry crumbled
And down Humpty tumbled.
Said the officer "You!
Get rid of that glue.
It's omelette for breakfast today!"

The Ugly Duckling's looking wan:
He's grown into an Ugly Swan!

Rab McTavish, piper braw,
Told the Magistrate "Awa'
Oor Tam wad nivver tak a pig,
So stick that underneath yer wig!"
The Magistrate said "Jock McLeod
Heard yon piggie squealing loud."
Said Rabbie "Och, it's as I feared,
'Twas nae the pig, 'twas my pipes he
    heer'd."

In a courtroom one day
We heard a Judge say
"You did what? Stuck a baby on top of a
    tree?"
And you got the impression
A complex depression
Approaching last Monday
From Biscay or Lundy
Dislodged the wee mite?"
(The defendants turned white)
"Yet you enter an innocent plea!
It's fifteen years each for the child you
    offended.
Like the baby, however, I'll make it
    suspended."

The COMPLETE WIT & WHIMSEY

"Rapunzel, Rapunzel, please let down your hair!"
As Sir Lancelot climbed up, he heard a great tear.
"I've gone bald" screamed the damsel, while blushing quite red,
"And my knight's on the ground there, bloody well dead.

Those of us blessed with children know that as they grow, year by year, they remain a major concern to us. But surely one day we can escape our parental responsibilities – can't we?

A FAMILY SONNET

Oh, children are a wond'rous gift,
They warm the heart, the spirit lift.
From first appearance in their prams
Until they pass their last exams
We nurture them, we watch them grow,
We tell them things they have to know.
But when at last away they drift
We tend to pleasure at the rift,
For now, at last, they all have grown
And (as we say) the nest have flown.
At last the burden moves away
And we have earned our holiday.

So let's relax, let's have a rest –
Oh God, it's Helen's driving test!

Part 2: IN LIGHTEST VEIN

Inevitably, as a diabetic (Type 2) here is a little whinge about getting diabetes. I'm now looking for some rhymes for coeliac!

A SUGAR-FREE SONNET

If you develop diabetes,
'Bye-bye chocolate, 'bye-bye sweeties.
It's no good cursing fickle Fate,
You must eschew that After Eight
And you must now consign to dreams
Those Hobnobs and those Custard Creams.
Apart from fruit, eat nothing sweeter
For your supper than Ryvita.
When shopping, be aware of diet:
The rule is - if it's wholemeal, buy it!
Oh, happy band of diabetics,
Your life is ruled by dietetics.

But listen - things could be much worse
Without your diabetic nurse!

When allergies come under discussion, this much-maligned little fellow often gets a mention.

ODE TO THE HOUSE - DUST- MITE

On your sheet, so lily white,
Lurks the tiny house-dust-mite.
He waits for you to go to bed
And takes up station near your head.
Then, when he thinks you're fast asleep,
Up your nostril he will creep
Where, being such a friendly species,
He leaves donations of his faeces.

The COMPLETE WIT & WHIMSEY

Lots of people like watching football, but did you know that insects also like watching it. And none more so than earwigs, as this little verse tells us.

THE EARWIG SUPPORTERS CLUB

Oh, earwigs they love to watch football,
They watch it both home and away.
They travel by train and they stand in the rain
And they come home the following day.

Some earwigs support Man. United,
While others like Crewe or Carlisle
And some find that Leeds will take care of their needs,
And one watches Plymouth Argyle.

Yes, earwigs they love to watch football.
You'll see them there, row after row,
And when there's a goal, they sing out of control
"Earwig oh, earwig oh, earwig oh!"

WHY PEOPLE WRITE POETRY

Some people love toads
And pen a few oads.
Sick men love nurses
And might write them vurses.

But most envy Seamus
And want to be
- Feamus,

Here is another of life's imponderables.

THE SNEEZE

A funny thing I've found with sneezes –
They always seems to come in threeses.
Not oneses, twoses, even fourses,
It must be one of Nature's lawses.
We have two feets, we have two kneeses,
But sneezes always comes in
Threeses.

Part 2: IN LIGHTEST VEIN

POEM FOR STEPHANIE

"Can I become famous in the literary world?"
"Yes, of course, Stephanie. Write a *modern* poem. Come on, I've told you how:
First, make sure there are no rhymes, no shape and no metre.
Use unrelated words in juxtaposition.
Coin neologisms. By the way that's tautology.
Think of a subject known to few.
Half way down your poem, insert a solitary word, preferably an adverb, like
Silently.
Include allusions to personal things like a holiday in Lyme Regis
Or people called Aubrey (rhymes with strawberry, but don't!).
Give your poem an eye-catching title, preferably in Latin.
Then clever people will study your poem and discourse earnestly upon it.

Good heavens, Stephanie, fourteen lines.
You've written a sonnet!

The COMPLETE WIT & WHIMSEY

Now I don't know about you, but I like good old traditional English food. OK, I quite like a pasta or a curry, but I also like meat and two veg. And when I say "two veg" I mean two proper veg, not these weird, weedy pretend veg that have crept in from somewhere, just to make the number up. Like baby corn! What possible good is that to man or beast? And the same for that other culinary nightmare: mange-tout. Whenever I see them, my feelings run high. In fact, something like the ones expressed in this poem, which is entitled "An Encounter With a Dish of Mange-tout". I hope you won't mind a few French words creeping in.

AN ENCOUNTER WITH A DISH OF MANGE-TOUT

Oh, green, pretentious bowl of slime,
You waste of money, waste of time.
I shun your texture, shun your stench,
Your need to be addressed in French.
You lie there, languid, limp and wet,
Emasculated, weak, effete.
My vegetables must be a treat,
Food fit for Englishmen to eat:
The proud potato, sturdy bean,
And cauliflower of lusty mien,
The firm young carrot, brawny beet,
With buxom Brussels, round and sweet,
Or muscled cabbage, swede of thew,
To chaperone a roast or stew,
And potent parsnip, lusty leek,
With broccoli of strong physique.
But you, just lying, sweating, there,
How can I countenance such fare?
Yet chefs who try to cause a stir:
Practitioners of *cordon bleu*
Consider you bring class and style
While I just think you're something vile!
Why must I eat you, pray? *Pourquoi?*
Emaciated *petit pois.*
Pour moi, cela ne va pas bien:
Ce n'est pas mange-tout, c'est mange rien!

Part 2: IN LIGHTEST VEIN

Jobs around the house are not my strong suit, but when I first had to get involved in them as a house-owner back in the 1960s, there seemed to be a conspiracy to make things even more complicated than they need have been. A second type of screw head suddenly appeared on the scene from nowhere and, whatever the job, I soon found I lacked the right sort and size of screwdriver. Why did this happen, except to cause amateurs like me endless frustration, and to make someone else a fat sum of money?

ALL SCREWED UP

Who is this Mr Phillips
Who makes me have to pay
For all those funny screwdrivers?
Who is this fellow, pray?
What made him spurn convention?
What made him shun the norm?
And torment unskilled amateurs
With screw-slots cruciform?

*

Now screws should all be standard,
I do not ask a lot,
Deep and wide from side to side
All screws should have one slot.
Not one that goes from north to south,
A second east to west.
Where there's this cross, I'm at a loss.
This Phillips chap's a pest!

*

Perhaps he was converted -
A modern-day St. Paul,
Who sought to bring the Christian faith
To pagans, one and all.
An engineering contest?
Competing for a cup?.
Whate'er the truth, friend Phillips,
You really screw me up!

The COMPLETE WIT & WHIMSEY

This poem is my tribute to a group of ladies I greatly admire, and who epitomise all that is great and noble in the British character (though they did let me down a little over that calendar!)

WI, OH WI

In the annals of our land
It's not hard to understand
Why, when set upon by Viking, Hun or Jute
We just take it on the chin
And come bouncing back to win:
Yes, the reason is the Women's Institute.

*

In our nation's darkest hour
When the French were made to cower
And when all our other neighbours followed suit,
Who provided inspiration
To our little island nation?
Why, the women of the Women's Institute.

*

When the bombs began to slam,
Who just kept on making jam,
Imperturbable among their mounds of fruit?
Who brought civilising skills
'Mid the dark satanic mills?
Why, the women of the Women's Institute.

*

They have quite outstanding morals,
And do not indulge in quarrels
   - They consider it unseemly to dispute.
They don't have romantic dreams,
They're not driven by extremes –
Not the women of the women's institute.

Part 2: IN LIGHTEST VEIN

They're polite and rather formal,
Their attire is plain and normal –
Just a skirt and jumper, twin set or a suit,
(Except when shocking vicars
By an absence of their knickers
For a calendar that many thought was cute.)

*

But despite these naughty pranks
They deserve our deepest thanks:
They're adorable, dependable, astute.
So let's give a loud ovation
To the backbone of our nation:
Those dear women of the Women's Institute!

The COMPLETE WIT & WHIMSEY

When I'm out somewhere with my wife, I sometimes drive. I'll say no more, but simply offer you this little poem entitled "My Satnav."

MY SATNAV

I have a little Satnav,
It sits there in my car.
A Satnav is a driver's friend.
It tells you where you are.

I have a little Satnav,
I've had it all my life.
It does more than a normal one:
My Satnav is my wife.

It gives me full instructions
On exactly how to drive.
"It's thirty miles an hour," it says,
"You're doing thirty-five."

It tells me when to stop and start
And when to use the brake,
And tells me that it's never ever
Safe to overtake.

It tells me when a light is red,
And when it goes to green
It seems to know instinctively
Just when to intervene.

It lists the vehicles just in front,
It lists them to the rear,
And taking this into account
It specifies my gear.

I'm sure no other driver
Has so helpful a device:
For when we leave and lock the car,
It still gives its advice.

It fills me up with counselling,
Each journey's pretty fraught.
So why don't I exchange it
And get a quieter sort?

Ah well, you see, it cleans the house,
Makes sure I'm properly fed.
It washes all my shirts and things
And – keeps me warm in bed!

CONTENTS

Which are the best years of your life? I ask this because there I was in this pub, minding my own business, when suddenly a crowd of locals began arguing about this very thing. I decided to dot down their arguments.

DECADE OF DELIGHT

As I sat in a country inn,
(A humble paying guest),
The local clan this row began:
Which decade was the best?
'Mid smoke and sound they sat around
Too close to be ignored,
While two old farts were playing darts
And chalking on a board.

A young man cried "Now look at me:
I've just escaped the teens.
I work all day, then time for play
And changing into jeans.
There's loads to do: there's girls to woo,
You've energy in plenty.
You're in your prime, you've got the time –
It's brilliant when you're 20!"

Another fellow said "Hold on.
I've been through all that mess:
You live like pigs in rundown digs
- You call that happiness?
You feed on chips and Instant Whips,
Your clothes are always dirty.
But now I'm wed (and clean and fed):
Thank God for reaching 30!"

A lady cried "Do not deride
The decade next in line.
The kids have grown, the nest they've
 flown,
My time at last is mine.
My footsteps stray to film or play
(Including some quite naughty),
And sometimes boys become your toys
When you get just past 40!"

Then up and spoke an older bloke:
"I took retirement early.
With hair still black I've turned my back
Upon the hurly-burly.
I left my trade with mortgage paid
(I've always been quite thrifty).
I'm free, I'm rich, I've got the itch
To sample life at 50!"

Then one old fart put down his dart
And said "You're wrong, you know.
Forget the rest, three score's the best,
I reached it years ago.
'Tis then you're blessed with time to rest,
While wisdom finds its peak.
And better yet, you're not a threat
To those who glory seek.

In these three ways you score the best:
That's why it's called three score,
This newborn stage, this golden age,
These sixties I adore.
Ah, well" said he, "I'll leave you be,
It's time for me to stop."
And, picking up his dart again,
He threw a treble top!

The COMPLETE WIT & WHIMSEY

What's in a name? Quite a lot if your parents chose first names which, used together with the last name, provoke mirth (I know a very nice lady called Theresa Green). The same can be said for first names which, reduced to initials and used with your last name, can also produce an unfortunate pairing, like I P Green. Hence this little poem.

INITIAL REACTION

Some Whitehall mandarins decreed
How best to serve the General Need:
The General Need would best be served
(These Whitehall mandarins observed)
If correspondence could be signed
With one thing uppermost in mind:
The need for informality.
That's what they wrote in their decree.

They said "Recipients don't spark
If signatures are bald and stark:
Initials on their own won't do,
So don't sign 'S' - sign 'Steve' or 'Sue'.
Sign 'Jean' or 'Jane', not 'J' - and never
Sign as 'T', write 'Tom' or 'Trevor'.
Managers will please insist
All staff comply (or slap their wrist)."

The Union, curiously, agreed
That this would serve the General Need
And even said they would endorse
In public such a noble course.
And so, as Conference approached,
The list of motions to be broached
Included one that underlined
How correspondence should be signed.

Proposers of the motion (viz:
Peter Nutt and Gary Whizz)
Said "Friends, initials really hurt you!"
"Hear! Hear!" said Elsie Christine Virtue.
And several others said their piece:
Brenda Keeney, Olive Beece,
And nobody was going to gag
Old Fred Luent, or Thomas Bagge.

The Chairman said "It's very clear
That no-one is dissenting here.
There's no doubt how the issue stands,
And no call for a show of hands."
But then a voice with passion cried
"Just wait and hear the other side."
A man and woman braved the crush.
They reached the stage and called for hush.

"Our name is Dover" said the man,
"My name is Ben, my wife here's Ann.
She's in the Inland Revenue.
I'm Education. So we two
Will use initials, by your leave.
To sign in full would be naïve."
Then, as the tongues began to wag,
Up spoke three more, from Min of Ag.

Part 2: IN LIGHTEST VEIN

Or Defra, as it's known today,
Said one "We need to have our say:
Let's use initials. They're much better.
I'm Mrs. Bunn, or Henrietta,"
The other said "I curse my fate:
My family name is Saturate.
I really wish I were a man,
My given names are Polly Ann."

The Chairman said "It seems to me
We'll not reach unanimity,
So I suggest we simply choose
The signature we each should use."
The meeting voted with one voice
That signing style be left to choice.
The Civil Service mandarins
Agreed, and took it on their chins.

In fact, they found it rather droll
(Except their boss, Sir Roger Sole.)

The COMPLETE WIT & WHIMSEY

Sadly, the Queen Mum has passed on now, but I wrote this little story when she was very much alive and kicking, and only in her early 90's! **The story may be a piece of fiction, but I think it's very much in the spirit of what she would love to get up to, given half the chance.**

FINESSING THE QUEEN

Oh, what a naughty lady: she'd played that trick before.
(In fact, she'd played it several times since 1984).
For she was getting on a bit when all was said and done,
So why not rearrange her life to have a little fun?
She loved to be with children, or watch the horses race,
Or sip some tea down by the sea, or in some country place.
Those endless royal engagements at last began to pall.
And military establishments - seen one, you'd seen them all!
Mind you, there used to be a time when Generals she'd beguile,
When Air Chief Marshalls got a wink, and Admirals a smile.

She had this friend called Maggie - in Wimbledon, I think,
A famous actress (now retired) who loved her food and drink.
Yes, Maggie loved the Good Life: *cuisine cordon bleu.*
If she were offered gourmet food, she never would demur.
And, as a former actress, she was mistress of disguise:
With just a bit of make-up, she'd transform before your eyes.

The Naughty Lady 'phoned her up one evening rather late:
"Oh, Maggie dear, it's Lizzie here, I've got another date."
So can you get those friends of yours to book that coach again,
And organise an outing? Right, now let me tell you when:
It's the twenty first of August...." And so they both agreed
To implement in deepest Kent their blueprint to mislead.
Then the Lady sent a letter to a military address,
Confirming she'd be happy to take luncheon in their Mess.

Because her destination really wasn't very far,
For this event the Lady went the whole way there by car.
No escort was provided as they prepared to go:
It wasn't cost-effective, so the Powers-That-Be said "No!"
The Lady-in-Attendance was a confidante most loyal:
A willing stooge to subterfuge and machinations royal.

Part 2: IN LIGHTEST VEIN

The driver left the orbital as he was bid to do,
Then very soon the Passenger said "Stop, please, at the loo."
Now there's a service station here ('tis dear old Clacket Lane),
Where people stop to eat and shop and shelter from the rain.
The driver walked them to the door, then had to leave them be:
He must eschew the Ladies' loo because he was a 'he'.
The Lady reappeared (he thought. He mustn't take the blame:
Old biddies wearing frilly hats look very much the same).

'Twas Maggie that the Lady-in-Attendance helped inside,
Then both, I think, exchanged a wink, and sat back for the ride,
While You-Know-Who got in the coach. They knew from whence she'd come,
This Lady wearing Maggie's clothes. So Maggie's friends kept Mum.

Then, when they reached the southeast coast and strolled beside the sands,
The Lady said "Now close your eyes, and all hold out your hands."
And, putting hand beneath her dress, produced a range of liquors:
(It's quite amazing what they'll hold - those knee-length granny knickers!)
And then they bought some fish and chips. They ate them as they walked.
Oh, what a lovely time they had: they ate, they drank, they talked.
They also had some dizzy rides upon the Roller Coaster,
Then played the darts and hoopla stalls: (the Lady won a toaster.)
They had a tipple in a pub. The tabloid press was there
In search of summer features, but the Lady didn't care.
Then it was time to start back home, though nobody was keen.
With smiles, with sighs, they closed their eyes, and sang of Nellie Dean.

Meanwhile, what price our Maggie, marooned in darkest Kent?
Well, truth to tell she did quite well right up until she went.
She puzzled them a little on arrival, saying "Thanks.
I'm glad you've asked me to inspect your boats - or is it tanks?"
And when she met the Commandant, a jolly, friendly sort,
She said "Oh, Brigadier's too long: I'll call you 'dear' for short."
They raised a teeny eyebrow at the seven gin and tonics,
Till someone said that's normal for the relatives of monarchs.
They also slightly wondered why she hung around till nine:
She should have left at five-ish, when the band played Auld Lang Syne.

The COMPLETE WIT & WHIMSEY

Eventually they said farewell. She told the Brigadier
"You've all been very kind to me, you'll get a Knighthood, dear."
At Clacket Lane they switched again and went their separate ways,
Each one quite buoyed: they so enjoyed these extra-special days.

Next day arrived a summons from The Daughter, sounding stern:
"Mother, dear, come over here. When will you ever learn?"
When she arrived, The Daughter said "Just look at all the papers:
'Knees-up For The Pensioners' and 'Grandmas Cutting Capers.'"
(They all wore silly seaside hats: hers said 'One gin, I'm yours.'
Their legs were kicked up high and showed their geriatric drawers.)
"Your conduct" said The Daughter, "Really cannot be excused.
As someone in this job before said 'We are not amused'.
If you keep playing childish games, well then eventually
The wretched Press are sure to guess, and stick you on Page 3.
If only I could be assured your naughty ways you'll mend,
I'd leave to you an Air Force do I find I can't attend."

The Lady said "I'll go instead. Now don't you worry, dear.
Just simply state the chosen date. Now, is it far from here?
The Daughter told her where it was, and also named the date.
Then, with a look inside a book, the Lady said "That's great!
I'll lend a hand, I've nothing planned, so all I need to do
Is tell my staff to run my bath at nine, or quarter to."

That evening Maggie had a 'phone call: "Want another lark?
Yes, super lunch An airfield, dear Not far from Kempton Park."

Part 2: IN LIGHTEST VEIN

This poem is best described as a conversation between a mother and her daughter, who, she is afraid, might be left on the shelf. Mama wants to make sure her daughter weds the right kind of man. But who is the right kind of man?

MOTHER KNOWS BEST

"Oh daughter, dear," her mother said,
You're twenty nine and not yet wed.
You're still as pretty as can be,
But that's because you look like me.
Now why not marry Harold More?
I know he's pushing fifty four,
And sweats a bit and likes to brag,
- But he's filthy rich and he drives a Jag.

*

"But mother dear, I've found my man:
He's tall and blonde with a lovely tan.
And though he's got this peculiar odour
You ought to see his vintage Skoda."

*

"Oh daughter, dear, you'll never learn.
You must judge men by what they earn,
And never let them go too far
Unless they drive an expensive car.
Though Harold More is rather dull,
And comes from just near Solihull,
And sometimes likes to dress in drag,
He's filthy rich and he drives a Jag."

*

"But mother, dear, I've found my man:
He lives with his mother in a caravan.
He's never paid back the money he owed her,
But you ought to see his vintage Skoda."

*

"Oh daughter, dear, to be a wife
Your man must keep you all your life.
It's not enough to hug and kiss,
It's money that brings you married bliss.
Though Harold More is rather fat,
His firm sells loads of this and that.
His shoulders droop and his buttocks sag,
But he's filthy rich and he drives a Jag."

*

"But mother dear, I've found my man:
He says he's the Chief of the Haggis Clan,
And though he loves his Scotch and soda,
You ought to see his vintage Skoda."

*

"So daughter, you won't make a match
With a man who's rich and is there to catch?
You'd rather have you're Skoda man
Who lives with his mother in a caravan.
Well, that's all right, I'll shed no tears.
See, I've been a widow for several years
And I had to ask to be quite sure:
For I plan to marry dear Harold More!"

Part 2: IN LIGHTEST VEIN

Here's anther bit of pure nonsense. If anyone inspired it, the blame would probably go to Lewis Carroll.

HERO OF OUR TIME

Oh, have you heard of Paddy,
A hero of our time?
Well, if you haven't heard of him
Just listen to my rhyme.

Now Paddy was a Welshman,
Who sailed the seven seas
From Liverpool to Birmingham
And round the Hebrides.

His boat was made of balsa wood,
The masts were made of steel.
He lived on bread and marmalade
And plates of jellied eel.

No man was born so debonair,
So clever and so strong:
He did the most courageous deeds
(But sometimes got them wrong).

At twelve o'clock in London Town
He climbed right up Big Ben.
He changed the time to ten past two
And then climbed down again.

He played full back for Arsenal
And seven goals he scored.
Each one was for the other side
So then he just got bored.

He went to Lords on Christmas Day
And strode out to the wicket.
As no-one else turned up to play
He won his game of cricket.

He rowed across to Calais
On a barrel of Champagne,
And said "Buon giorno" to the French,
Who said "Auf Wiedersehn."

And when they pointed out his faults,
He vowed he'd get things right,
So found his boat at close of day,
And sailed at dead of night.

He'd heard about a kidnapping
And found the villain's lair.
He wrote his plan on marzipan
To get them out of there.

He took the villain by surprise,
And in his daring raid
He saved a fearsome dragon
From a sweet and gentle maid.

So now you've heard of Paddy,
A hero bold and strong,
Who did the most courageous deeds
(But sometimes got them wrong).

The COMPLETE WIT & WHIMSEY

I was invited to give recitals to a few home-made wine clubs, and I wrote this little poem for them. I was, in fact, a keen wine-maker myself in my younger days, when I couldn't afford to go to the pub. This was in the days before grape concentrates appeared on the scene, and all the ingredients were plucked from the garden, the hedgerow or …anywhere.

HOME BREW

When Fred came out the Rose and Crown
He cried "That's dreadful stuff!"
And said to Ern with features stern
"I'm glad I've had enough."
Then pretty soon old Ernie said
"If you don't like this pub
Then listen, Fred, let's join instead
That wine and social club.

"Oh, yes" said Fred, "I think I read
They meet each Wednesday night
To have a chat on this and that
Then go home nice and tight.
They've got to be like you and me,
I think we'd fit in fine,
And there isn't much with yeast and such
You can't turn into wine."

So join they did for fifteen quid
And very quickly found
Just what you do to make a brew
With anything around.
So Fred dug up his garden veg
And chopped them up real fine,
Then boiled the lot in pan and pot
And turned them into wine.

And when he'd pluck'd the garden clean
He thought "Where shall I go?
The hedgerows seem to fit my scheme
With hip and haw and sloe.

They grow and grow *fortissimo*
Like grapes upon the vine,
And there isn't much with yeast and such
You can't turn into wine.

"And now" said Fred, "The garden shed -
I'll bet there's something there."
And sure enough he found some stuff
Like cast-off underwear,
And one old welly ripe and smelly
Some fag-ends and some twine
And he added a quart of prunes he'd bought
And he turned it into wine.

Then his missus said "Now listen, Fred,
While you were out tonight
I thought I'd go and see our Flo
And got an awful fright.
She wasn't there, the house was bare."
Said Fred "My sister's fine,
I took her out for a walkabout
And a glass of me home-made wine.

I like a brew and Flo does, too,
And the one she loves to drink
Is the one I make from dried-up cake
I make it in the sink.
Just add a bit o' kitty-litter,
Mash it nice and fine
And you've got the queen of the whole cuisine -
The finest home-made wine."

God moves in mysterious ways to show us His will, like plonking a pimple on Milady! Or was it a pimple?

VOCATION

Lady Amanda Dalrymple
On her forehead had such a large pimple.
So, when people mocked her
She summoned the doctor,
Said "Please cut it off."
But he gave a short cough,
Said "Milady, it's not quite that simple.

To begin with, your pimple's a wart.
(It's probably something you caught).
What you need's a magician
And not a physician,
Or someone who sells
Incantations and spells
If you wish to reduce it to nought."

So she looked through the thick Yellow Pages,
She took it in logical stages:
'Phoned each water-diviner
(Both major and minor)
And witches and wizards
(And a man who bred lizards).
It took her just ages and ages.

But no-one could help Lady A.
So she said to herself 'I must pray.
It's God I must ask
To take on this task
And give me advice.'
And then, in a trice,
The Almighty One showed her the way.

So Lady Amanda Dalrymple
Came to terms with her wart (erstwhile pimple):
She travelled to Kerry,
Joined the Sisters of Mary.
Now she grins at her wart,
For, just as God taught,
She covers it up with her wimple!

The COMPLETE WIT & WHIMSEY

We're back with the Nursery Rhymes again!

REVENGE OF THE MICE

Three mice, with dark glasses and canes,
Came searching for breakfast remains.
But the farmer's wife saw them
(Could hardly ignore them),
Gave the scream of her life
And seized a sharp knife,
Thought 'They can't see a lot o' me
So a rear-end lobotomy
Will alter their features
And frighten the creatures
And cause them some pain.
They'll not come back again!'

So she grabbed each intruder in turn
By the tip of his browny-grey stern.
With a slice quick and deft
Each was swiftly bereft
Of his beautiful tail.
They escaped with a wail,
Made it back to their nest,
Where their loved ones, distressed,
Shedding copious tears,
Neatly bound up their rears.
Then, with unison squeak
Cried "Revenge we must seek!"

So the mice held a Council of War
And plotted to even the score:
"We can't get the wife,
She's larger than life.
But we can get her cat.
Yes! How about that!"
To avoid a collision
They chose mice with good vision,
And with some trepidation
They took up their station.
On nocturnal foray
They watched for their quarry.

The cat yawned when he'd had his cat-nap
And barged his way through the cat-flap.
As he strolled past the leeks,
With belligerent squeaks
Six mice quickly sat on him,
Immediately flattened him,
Chopped his tail off with ease
And escaped through the trees.
Twenty days the cat ran
To the Island of Man,
Where he caused a sensation

And fathered a nation!

Part 2: IN LIGHTEST VEIN

I often write poems for family occasions, and to mark my niece's marriage I wrote two poems, one each for the bride and groom.

WEDDING DAY PRAYERS

They went to church and made a vow.
The wedding feast is over now.
We see them kneeling in their room,
A nervous, anxious bride and groom.
They've both been taught each night to pray;
Let's listen in to what they say.
First, here's the bride, so sweet and pure,
Devout, delightful and demure.

THE BRIDE'S PRAYER

"Dear Lord, I thank you for my groom,
A man to sit with in my room.
Please make him brave, with shoulders broad,
So that he can protect me, Lord,
Each time I see a savage mouse
Or hairy spider in the house.
Please put wise counsel in his head
And let him never snore in bed.
Oh, may he never smell of drink,
And teach him to unblock a sink.
Oh, please make sure he never bores me,
Tells me always he adores me,
And when I need a brand-new dress,
Teach him, Lord, to acquiesce
And, as the years go rolling by,
 Keep me the apple of his eye."

And now, continuing our plan,
 Let's hear the groom, a fine young man:

THE GROOM'S PRAYER

"Dear Lord, I thank you for my bride,
A mate to live with, side by side.
Teach her, Lord, each wifely duty
And please preserve her youthful beauty.
Though I'm grateful for those looks,
Make her, Lord, the best of cooks.
Keep her loving, never cold,
Quick to praise and slow to scold.
And if I have a little thirst
Let her not suspect the worst.
And if I go out with the boys
Make her deaf to all my noise.
Please teach her how to act in bed
To make me warm from toe to head.
And keep her, Lord, as time goes by,
Serene, obedient, chaste and shy,

Their duty done, their prayers all said,
The couple shyly climb to bed.
So now let's tiptoe from the room,
And leave the rest to bride and groom!
Theirs is the hardest task in life:
Learning to be man and wife!

Part 2: IN LIGHTEST VEIN

Anyone for Bridge? I love the game, so not surprisingly I've written a few poems centred around it. For those of you not familiar with Bridge, I should explain that it's a card game which is very easy except for two things: the bidding and the card play. The bidding is a sort of coded dialogue you have with your partner to agree on how many tricks you can make together if a certain suit is trumps, or if there are no trumps. And, having declared your intention, you then set out to do this by playing the cards while your opponents try to stop you succeeding. Here at last is a poem for the thousands of Bridge players who have endured heart surgery – well, Geoffrey anyway. Those of you who do play Bridge will understand why the poem is entitled

MAKING ONE HEART NON-VULNERABLE

Geoffrey Peters, Bridge fanatic,
Self-effacing, enigmatic,
One day felt a sort of hurt
From somewhere underneath his shirt,
The doc said "Sorry, Mr P.
You're going to need some surgery:
It's time your ticker had a service,
It's quite routine, so don't be nervous."
He gazed into his doctor's crystal
And said "There's room for you in Bristol."

So down the M5 motorway
Went Geoffrey on the chosen day
And waited shyly, like a virgin,
For the designated surgeon.
The Great Man came and looked around
(While all about him kissed the ground)
- A brilliant man, a man with brains,
Who said "I'm going to need some veins.
I need to see which leg to choose
So please remove your socks and shoes."

The time came for the operation.
Each stood at his appointed station,
While Geoffrey on his back they laid.
The surgeon seized his trusty blade.
Procedures? He'd no need to learn 'em
(As long as you could find the sternum)

Because he had his Book of Rules
The one you get at Doctors' Schools.
So, in the Index near the start
He found the chapter labelled "Heart".

Then, glancing at the television,
He made a confident incision,
And with a manner most becoming
Wrestled with aortal plumbing.
At last, with triumph on his face,
He delicately sewed in place
The final vein, the final widget,
(While Geoffrey didn't even fidget).
The surgeon said "Right, time for grub"
And cleared off to the nearest pub.

At first recovery was slow
And Geoffrey felt extremely low.
With bowel and appetite on "Stop"
He wished he'd never had the op.
And then they said he'd better dress
And go on home to convalesce.
Then hairy men in hairy clothes
With rings through ears, and rings
    through nose
Arrived and camped upon his lawn
And slept in trees from dusk to dawn.

The COMPLETE WIT & WHIMSEY

The crowd became two hundred strong
The Police moved in among the throng
And said "'Ello, 'ello, 'ello
What's all this 'ere, we'd like to know."
The campers said "We've had a tip
From people in our leadership.
They've sent us here to demonstrate:
Some problems with a by-pass, mate.
And so we're going to camp out here
In case the diggers should appear.

When Geoffrey disabused the herd
They all dispersed without a word.
And soon his appetite increased -
He wouldn't eat, he'd simply feast!
The doctor said "This op, I find,
Improves the body and the mind.
Your Bridge will much improve. You'll see.
So Geoffrey (slick at repartee)
Said "Come on, Doc, you must be kidding:
I'll never fathom Christine's bidding!"

This was my first Bridge poem. It takes us into the genteel world of the Ladies' Bridge group, where, in a very civilised setting, they all take their turn to host the event.

THE BRIDGE PARTY

'Twas mother's turn to host the Bridge:
Cheese and pâté in the fridge.
She knew exactly what they ate
At Party Bridge and Duplicate.

As she began to serve the snack
Arnold came in at the back,
Rushed upstairs to take a shower
After jogging for an hour.

He stripped right off, then gave a howl
"Mother, where's the blooming towel?"
Barged straight in, completely nude.
Mother said "That's very rude,
Especially when I'm serving food."

The ladies of the Bridge Club stared
As Arnold his credentials bared.
"Goodness me" thought three old maids,
'A gorgeous lad - and that's in spades!"

Part 2: IN LIGHTEST VEIN

Apart from drawing-room Bridge, where "Rubber" Bridge is usually played by just four people who continually deal the cards for every game, most good players belong to a Club, where usually several dozen players assemble and the order of the day is Duplicate Bridge. Here, all the hands are dealt at the start and each table plays its initial allocation of three or four deals. The hands are then preserved in special wallets and are passed to the next table. Some of the players will also move in a pre-arranged order, so that at the end of the session, everyone will eventually have played the same hands. The basic playing unit is the pair, and in some competitions two pairs play as a team and aggregate their scores. Sorry about all this verbiage, just to introduce a silly Bridge limerick!

A BRIDGE LIMERICK

A Bridge-playing lady called Claire
Was so gorgeous that men used to stare.
The bit that was best
Was right there on her chest:
 - The most beautiful duplicate pair!

This was my winning entry for the Valentine Competition run by the magazine "Bridge Plus" in 1996. I think a limit was imposed, like 50 words.

MY BRIDGE VALENTINE

Oh, wise of mind and round of rump,
Who rescues me from One No Trump
And, knowing what a child I am,
Entrusts to me each certain slam,
Let's share a contract meant for life:
Dear heart, I bid you, be my wife.

The COMPLETE WIT & WHIMSEY

I sometimes like trying to capture the style of other poets, and one of my favourites is Sir John Betjeman, the people's poet. I'm sure we're all familiar with such gems as "Come friendly bombs and fall on Slough, It isn't fit for humans now..." and the Subaltern's Love-Song about the couple who fall in love playing in a tennis tournament: "Miss Joan Hunter-Dunn, Miss Joan Hunter-Dunn, Furnish'd and burnish'd by Aldershot sun ..." Well, this little poem of mine transfers these sentiments away from the tennis court to the Bridge table. It's called "Cards on the Table."

CARDS ON THE TABLE

Tricky the hands in the cardroom this evening.
The Brigadier's playing with dear Mrs Smythe,
And I am the partner of beautiful Angela,
Elegant, perky, intelligent, lithe.

One No-Trump, Two No-Trumps, Three No-trumps partner,
You had to keep bidding with so much to spare.
I know it's a risk with that silly old void
But a suitable lead and we're sure to be there.

Well, five down and doubled, I thought you did wonderfully,
Jolly bad luck that they had all the spades,
And the Brigadier – well, he's a trifle aggressive:
It comes from commanding those Army brigades.

Seven Hearts, partner, I do like your bidding.
Your singleton trump was – a sort of surprise.
They've doubled again, but they've got to be kidding:
I'll bring home this contract in front of your eyes.

Well, never mind, partner. Look, Saturday evening
Please come round to my place. Together we'll dine,
And after we've eaten there's Mozart and Scrabble
And After Eight mints and the rest of the wine.

At Bridge your performance is bold and commanding:
You play with great intellect, courage and style,
But Scrabble is mentally much more demanding
And – where did you get such a beautiful smile?

PART 3: Limericks, Non-Limericks and the Classics Revisited… Oh, and a few Clerihews

I consider the Limerick to be an art form that is seriously undervalued. It is one of the most challenging forms of verse to write well. You have five lines in which to introduce someone with a particular name or from a particular place, develop their character, create a story about them, and end with a punch line! I've written Limericks for at least the last 60 years. Sadly (for me) most got discarded after serving their purpose. Here are well over a hundred relatively recent ones followed by a few snippets not too dissimilar.

Monet to Renoir once said
"Let's do something different instead:
I suggest lots and lots
Of squiggles and dots,
Mainly in green and in red.

All the ladies in olden-day Phrygia
Suffered from steatopygia.
This means that their rump
Was inclined to be plump.
(That's something you didn't know, did ya?)

A cricket fanatic from Devon
Said, on admission to Heaven,
"If your first team's too strong
Then I hope before long
I'll be picked for the Second Eleven."

There was a young lady named Belle,
Who dreamt that she went down to Hell.
She met monsters like Hitler
(Some bigger, some littler)
And, strangely, Aunt Edith as well.

A slovenly maid from Westminster
Seemed resigned to the life of a spinster,
Till a policeman on duty
Discovered her beauty
(After he'd washed her and rinsed her.)

A lady from Berwick-on-Tweed
Is rather well known for her greed.
Take her dancing, that's fine,
But don't take her to dine
For the lady won't 'eat', she'll just 'feed'.

There was a large man from Dundee,
Who, naked, leapt into the sea.
He cried "I'm sae glad
I'm a braw Scottish lad!"
And he wobbled his buttocks in glee.

A brilliant young cellist named Hilda
Said Elgar's concerto just thrilled her,
But there wasn't much dough
In becoming a pro,
So she married a self-employed builder.

A motor-mechanic named Anna
Had a rather belligerent manner:
If a fellow spoke ill
Of her technical skill,
She'd loosen his nuts with a spanner.

A merchant who lived in Jakarta
Went into the market to bartar.
He bought for a maid
Some lovely brocade
For a clandestine glimpse of her garter.

The COMPLETE WIT & WHIMSEY

There is a sweet maid in our street,
Whose figure is shapely and neat,
But no husband she's won,
For when we get sun ...
Well, it has this effect on her feet.

In Zimbabwe (once Northern Rhodesia)
New-born babes have severe alopecia:
This is cured, it is said,
By immersing the head
In whisky and Milk of Magnesia.

We are grateful to Samuel Pepys,
For his diaries have given us hepys
Of historical facts
On the words and the acts
Of statesmen, of kings and of crepys.

There was a young lady called Sue,
Leaving school couldn't think what to do.
So she looked at her Mother
And then at her brother,
And applied for a job in a zoo.

A foolish young lady from Lincoln
Spent her evenings in clandestine drinking.
She once had a nose
That was white as a rose,
But she's now got a blue, green and pink 'un.

A rancher who lived near Seattle
In the Second World War went to battle:
He helped the advance
Through Belgium and France
By the timely stampede of his cattle.

There was a young lady from Riga,
Whose personal hygiene was meagre.
She ignored soap and water,
Instead, once a quarter,
She'd swab herself down with Swarfega.

A betrothed motor-cyclist called Trevor
His engagement to Ruth had to sever,
For his girl in a million
Fell right off his pillion,
But he rides on, more ruthless than ever.

There once was a great chef called Hugh
Who, unnoticed, fell into his stew.
It was done to a T
Though we had to agree
That it certainly had a strange hue.

There was a plump maiden from Dorset,
Who purchased a new-fangled corset.
But the first day she wore it
Her Mum said "You tore it.
If it won't all go in dear, don't force it!"

When an actress, who comes from Uttoxeter,
Plays Juliet, the audience mocks at her.
When she says "Wherefore art.."
Then they usually start
Throwing stink-bombs and old pairs of socks at her.

Years ago, all the ladies from Brussels
Wore dresses with elegant bustles.
But they soon got displaced,
Ended up round the waist,
After strenuous amorous tussles.

There was a young fellow from Bristol,
Who bought a clairvoyancy crystal.
He'd the shock of his life
As he saw his dear wife
Buying arsenic, some knives and a pistol.

A nagging old wife from Cologne
Once choked on a halibut bogne.
Her husband admired
The way she expired
And smiled as she gave her last grogne.

Part 3: LIMERICKS ETC

There was a young lady called Ethel,
Who often drank spirits of methyl.
If the things that she'll say
Won't give her away,
You can bet your sweet life that her breath'll.

At cards I join in with a will,
Though there are certain card games that still
Induce me to nap -
So you see there's a gap
That Nap will not bridge, but Bridge will.

A lady from Ballyjamesduff
At culture was bally game stuff.
To learn Chinese she tried
But eventually sighed
"Goodness me, aren't these bally names tough!"

There was a young lady from Sunderland
Whom her friends vowed they never could understand,
For each evening in bed
She'd stand on her head
And read extracts from Alice in Wonderland.

A Colonel from old Pondicherry
Found no gin in the mess, so drank sherry
Which, combined with the heat,
Knocked him clean off his feet
And, thus weakened, he caught beriberi.

An eccentric professor from Cheltenham
Amassed pieces of scrap, and by meltin' 'em
He made three pairs of boots
And two thin metal suits.
How uncomfortable he must have felt in 'em.

There was a young man from Porthcawl,
Who had no ambition at all.
Out loud he would cry
"On my bed will I lie
And stare all day long at the wall."

There was a young beauty from Turkey,
Who was charming, vivacious and perky.
She's such a delight
That her future looks bright -
Though her past is incredibly murky!

There was a young fellow from Fife
Who thought that he'd take him a wife.
So he tried one or two
And found they wouldn't do,
But he's having the time of his life.

An ugly old spinster named Jane
Every night walked alone down a lane,
Till a fellow from Gloucester
Jumped out to accost her
And vowed he'd not do so again.

A classical chap from Prestatyn
One day wore a suit made of satin.
When he heard how the crowd
Rudely mocked him out loud
He swore at the bastards in Latin.

A girl from the Forest of Dean
To do poses for money was keen.
She'd earn at her peak
Fifteen hundred a week -
Not bad for a kid of fourteen!

An adventurous fellow from Rome
Went travelling over the foam.
But the gay dilettante
Soon yearned for Chianti,
So quickly turned round and sailed home.

The COMPLETE WIT & WHIMSEY

There was a sweet maid from Odessa,
To their lips all the comrades would press her.
But to aid Perestroika
She eloped in a troika
With an old economics professor.

There was a young man from Brazil,
Took an innocent maid up a hill.
But her pa did discover
The name of her lover,
Said "Señor, please make out your will."

There was a young maiden from Bangor,
Whom a pilot once took to a hangar.
Spurred on by the screams
From jet flying machines,
'Twas there that she dropped her first clanger.

There was a young fellow from Preston,
To his girl made a naughty suggestion:
He said "Darling, tonight
Come round for a bite,
I'll just have my pants and my vest on."

There was a young maiden called Gert,
Reputed to be quite a flirt.
She charmed every he
With her slick repartee
And the twenty-inch slit in her skirt.

There was a young siren named Vera,
So passionate men used to fear her.
When she came into sight
They screamed out in fright
"For God's sake don't come any nearer!"

A corpulent maid from Malaya
Decided to make her life gayer.
So she hired two squads
Of fully trained bods
Each evening to strip her and weigh her.

There was a young lady from Lympne,
Who, last summer, decided to slympne.
She ate no food at all
And so, by the Fall
We were singing her funeral hympne.

There was a young lady called Janet,
Who did poses at theatres in Thanet.
Old men got a thrill
Every evening until
The magistrates stepped in to ban it.

A sailor from old Casablanca
Once got a job on a tanker.
He smoked below deck,
Now the ship is a wreck
(There are some who avow that he sank her.)

A nagging old woman from Slough
With her husband each day had a rough
Till at last, one fine day
It drove him away.
I'm sure that he's better off nough.

A large female wrestler called Brenda
Was at ease with the opposite gender:
She gave orders all day,
Which they leapt to obey
For fear they might somehow offend her.

A young tattooed lady named Bridget
Married the circus's midget.
Imagine the sauce -
He sued for divorce
On the grounds that his wife was too frigid.

A very posh lady from Stroud
Was terribly, terribly proud,
Till one evening at tea
In select company
She made a rude noise right out loud.

CONTENTS

There was a young chippie from Rhyl,
Who sat on a rather fierce drill:
He's had some problem sitting,
He's taken up knitting
And he's changing his first name to Lil.

A fellow from old Birkenhead
Would always eat biscuits in bed,
Till his wife cried "This trick
Just makes me feel sick!"
And she emptied her crisps on his head.

There was a vain lady named Polly,
Whose friends said she looked melancholy.
Explained her friend Helen
"Your head's like a melon,
And the rest of you looks like a collie."

There was a fair maiden from Leicester,
Whom gentlemen often would pester,
But now every day
She keeps them at bay
By wearing a grotty sou'wester.

There was a young fellow named Joe,
On the Lottery won lots of dough,
But he soon spent this sum
On whisky and rum
And a lady the Police know as 'Flo'.

There was a sweet maiden named Molly
Who went with a man to pick holly.
She felt all aglow
In spite of the snow,
And soon paid the price of her folly.

In the pulpit stood Father Maguire,
Searching for words to inspire,
But he got in a fluster
And all he could muster
Was verbal abuse of the choir.

The Minister rose from his place -
A figure of style and of grace.
As he started to speak,
His knees went all weak
And he promptly fell flat on his face.

The last time I went to Botswana
All the natives addressed me as "bwana".
This went to my head
Until somebody said
It's Swahili for rotten banana.

It's a shame about poor little Eleanor:
In spite of the things we keep tellin' her
She will wear perfume
That's cut-price, we presume,
And from 25 yards you start smellin' her.

A rather strange butcher from York
Took a sudden aversion to pork,
So in letters quite big
He wrote "Don't eat dead pig!"
Then he crunched up and swallowed the chalk.

An actress, who comes from Montrose,
Has starred in a good many shows,
And her future seems bright
For, after tonight,
She's been offered a part wearing clothes.

A missionary fellow from Brighton
Went to China, the hordes to enlighten,
But his message of Hell,
And Damnation as well
Served not to convert, but to frighten.

A Socialist priest from Cape Cod
Held views that were really quite odd:
He just gave Communion
To those in the Union
And said he was guided by God.

The COMPLETE WIT & WHIMSEY

There was an old man from Penzance
Whose house was infested with ants.
When he dug up their nest
He said "Just as I guessed:
They've come through a tunnel from France!"

A farmer's young daughter called Kay
Went for a romp in the hay.
She got straw up her rump
And her tummy got plump:
So, all in all, not a good day.

There was a young maid from Dubai,
Who hung out her knickers to dry,
But a dirty old sheikh
Round the corner did sneak
And grabbed them with glee in his eye.

Said the Boss to a girl from High Wycombe
"Here's two hundred stamps. Get and lick 'em!
He started to shout
"This post must go out!"
So she told him just where he could stick 'em.

For Christmas a lady called Tiffany
Had a negligée, flimsy and chiffony.
It was sexy and thin,
Felt so good on her skin
That she kept the thing on till Epiphany.

A silly young fellow called Kerr
In Cheltenham Spa caused a stir:
He stripped to his shoes,
Then drank lots of booze,
And the rest of the day was a blur.

Quite close to the centre of Wemys
There's an inn that has old-fashioned bemys.
'Twas there that young Tam,
After taking a dram
Proposed to the girl of his dremys.

A surgeon named Anne cried "Enough!
Just being accepted is tough.
I've patched up the heart
Of this stupid old fart
And he calls me a nice bit of stuff.

There was a young housewife from Reading,
Who paused as she shook out the bedding.
To the bathroom she crept
Where she silently wept
Over promises made at her wedding.

Noses dear? Have you seen Hilary's?
Covered in broken capillaries,
Caused without doubt
By her liking for stout
And the output of certain distilleries.

Thought Tracey "I'd love to elope,
But I don't think there's very much hope.
I know if he met me
He'd never forget me,
But he'd put his job first, being Pope."

There's a dish on the island of Ure
Made from cod, which they fix on a skewer;
Then they add a few shrimp,
Some firm and some limp,
And garnish with seagull manure.

Part 3: LIMERICKS ETC

A young courting couple from Norway
Were seen having fun in a doorway.
The lady said "Sven,
When we try this again
Then let's do things my way, not your way."

There once was a poet called Dylan,
Who tends to be cast as a villain.
I adored every word
Though it got rather blurred
On account of the booze he kept spillin'.

There was a young curate from Filey,
Whom the clergy regarded quite highly
Till he took that short break
For his grandfather's wake.
Now he's living the life of Old Reilly.

Said a very rich person from India
"There's no doubt that it's very much windier.
That means the monsoon
Will be here very soon,
So that's three months of Scrabble and gin, dear."

There was a young fellow from Hull,
Who found life in that town rather dull.
So for thrills, can you guess?
Yes, he's taken up chess
And writes poetry when there's a lull.

An elegant lady from Ayr
Always dressed with such style and such flair.
She loved the allure
Of the best haute-couture,
But beneath it all, well - she was bare.

When Santa Claus went to Bordeaux,
All the children got lots of *cadeaux,*
Then he leapt on his sleigh
And flew swiftly away,
With a wave and a cheery *heaux-heaux*!

A young Stone-Age fellow called Og,
Sat musing one day on a log.
He thought "Tapeworm I've got,
But fleas I have not,
So I think I'll domesticate Dog."

There was a sweet maid from Carlisle,
Who had the most beautiful smile.
When she took some fresh air
Folk would stand still and stare
While the traffic backed up for a mile.

Said a potty professor from Crewe
"There's some serious things I must do.
I must do a big sum
To show Springtime has come,
And why the sky always is blue."

A scholarly fellow from Caius
Felt a rather cold blast round the knaius.
"This building" he laughed,
"Has a terrible draught,
One minute you're hot, then you fraius!"

A sickly old cripple from Kent
Had a problem with paying the rent,
So the Council said "Oy!
You've been a bad boy,
You can bloody well live in a tent!"

There was an old sadist from Wells,
Who managed a chain of hotels
In those that were cheap
When you'd just got to sleep
They'd wake you with whistles and bells.

The COMPLETE WIT & WHIMSEY

A flat-chested girl from Dunbar
Put an egg in each cup of her bra.
Though the two sides now matched
The stupid eggs hatched.
Now there's chicks that regard her as Ma.

A passionate lady called Ella
Goes looking each day for a feller,
But she really won't mind
If a man she can't find
For she keeps a supply in the cellar.

A naturist couple from Tring
Go nude on the first day of Spring.
They walk round their land
With a twig in each hand
- It's just some fertility thing.

From their beds slip the ladies of Fakenham
(They do it from choice, no-one's makin' 'em).
They cavort until four
While their husbands all snore,
Then they sneak back to bed without wakin' 'em.

A certain French student wrote *"Le*
Invitation you sent me, Sir, *de*
Come for coffee or tea,
Well, the answer is *oui,*
With the greatest of pleasure, signed *je."*

A dirty young fellow from Leeds
Once fell in a barrel of seeds.
He's got golden crysanths
Growing out of his pants
And his nostrils are bunged up with weeds.

There once was a fellow named Ned,
Who wished his rich uncle was dead,
So he poisoned his tea,
Shot him five times with glee
And finally chopped off his head.

There was a sweet maid from Devizes,
Whose beauty would never win prizes:
She'd spots by the million,
Her nose was vermillion
And her teeth were all shapes and all sizes.

A Communist maiden named Clara
Was beautiful – no girl was fairer,
But she cannot get wed
For the Party, instead,
Has decreed all the workers must share her.

A young City fellow named Bertie
To the office went wearing no shirtie.
When his Boss asked him why
He was forced to reply
I'm sorry, they're all far too dirty."

There once was a strongman called Brian,
Who used to chew bars made of iron.
He could lift with one hand
A truck filled with sand
- And that was without really tryin'.

There was a young lady called Lil,
Who complained that she felt rather ill,
But the Doc put her right
By prescribing each night
Some Scotch and a green-coloured pill.

Part 3: LIMERICKS ETC

There was a young fellow from Deal,
Who had twenty-inch biceps of steel,
He's a fifty-inch chest,
Sixteen stone in his vest
- I think that it's called sex-appeal.

I met a poor woman from Neath,
Who had a disease of the teeth.
She could not eat her dinner,
Each day she got thinner,
And now we are laying a wreath.

I once knew a lady called Laura,
So ugly, all men would ignore her
Till she once met in Rhyl
A man uglier still
And doesn't this chap just adore her!

Another young lady called Laura
In bed was a terrible snorer,
But she cured her affliction,
Got rid of the friction
By swallowing dollops of Flora.

There was a young fellow named Louis
Who his friends thought was really quite screwy.
For the foolish young lad
Spent what money he had
On consistently drinking Drambuie.

There was a young Fräulein called Gretel,
Who scalded her bum on a kettle,
But the Doc soothed the place
Beneath layers of lace
And now she's in very fine fettle.

There was a young lady from Bruges,
Whose cheekbones were hollow and huge,
But, not lacking in teachers,
She doctored her features
With liberal layers of rouge.

A sweet little creature called Mary
Was employed as a maid in a dairy.
She'd a dear little face
And wore satin and lace
- What a pity her legs were so hairy.

There was a young fellow from Bolton
Who often ate crisps with no salt on.
A friend said "I'll bet on it
Old Charlie has sweat on it
For sweat, after all, is salt molten".

There was a young man from Port Said,
Who thought that his wife was a red,
For his beautiful darlin'
Had a picture of Stalin
Stuck up on the wall near their bed.

There was a young lady called Helen,
Who sailed to the Straits of Magellan.
She lived off raw fish,
Which she ate from a dish
With a couple of slices of melon.

A fellow from old Lanzarotte
Slept only with upper-class totty
A queen, two tsarinas
And four ballerinas
And the Duchess of Devonshire's Scotty.

A healthy young fellow from Luton
Fell ill when he swallowed a crouton.
He was very soon dead
And the Coroner said
"Poor chap was allergic to gluten".

A lovely young girl from Dun Laoghaire
Was gorgeous – no maiden was faoghaire.
Many avowed
She was better endowed
Than all the sweet colleens in Aoghaire.

The COMPLETE WIT & WHIMSEY

The Irish enjoy a good ceilidh,
With everyone acting quite geilidh.
If you play your cards right
And don't get in a fight
You'll find you can get to one deiligh.

NON-LIMERICKS

The policeman rushed into the ward
And grabbed an old man by the chest.
"I see you've come" the doctor said,
"To make a cardiac arrest."

The golfer had a super round.
He really had a lot of fun.
He then went home to change his socks
Because he'd got a hole in one.

The Sultan threw his wife into the sea,
The reason being that he wished to drown her.
On that date, 'twas no figment, all could see
A sultana raisin' currents all around her.

THE CLASSICS REVISITED

In Xanadu did Kubla Khan
A stately pleasure dome decree,
Where Alf and Bert, and cousin Stan
Did slide shows of the Isle of Man,
And then poured out the tea.

The curfew tolls the knell of parting day,
The weary herd winds slowly o'er the lea,
And Sharon loves that bloke across the way.
It's Blackburn 1 and Man United 3.

Hail to thee, blithe spirit,
Bird thou never wert,
(I'm sorry if I called you that:
It must have been that skirt.)

I must go down to the sea again,
To the lonely sea and the sky,
And see if that blonde's still hanging around,
That one that gave George that black eye.

Oh, young Lochinvar is come out of the west,
In his socks and his Y-Fronts, and wearing a vest.

CLERIHEWS

The Reverend Ian Paisley
Banged his fist and shouted crazily
"Dese bloddy Catholics make me sick.
T'ank God I'm not a red-faced Mick!"

Tony Blair
With his usual flair,
Agreed to stand down
And bequeath his mess to Brown.

Gordon Brown,
As soon as Blair stood down,
Said "I'll increase this ------ing deficit."
That blank isn't something beginning with 'f', is it?

Part 4: IN MORE SERIOUS VEIN

PART 4: In More Serious Vein

Among the more "serious" poems I have written, are number recalling my childhood before and during World War 2.

I was born in 1933 into the Army – at the Military Hospital in Colchester, in fact. Dad was a regular soldier and at the time of my birth, he was serving with the Royal Signals in Shanghai, and I didn't meet him until I was three. For those first three years of my life, while he was abroad, we lived with his parents, who kept a pub deep in the Suffolk countryside, an old-style spit and sawdust establishment. Grandpa Rafferty was a former soldier himself, a military mounted policeman who was born in Scotland of Irish parents. When he left the Army he worked as a groom on the Arundel Estate, re-enlisted for World War 1, was invalided out, then went into the pub trade. He doted on me and on my brother who was 2 years older. We had a wonderful time helping Grandpa run the pub, as we thought. Just up the road lived my mother's parents in a very old, tiny cottage with two great attractions nearby - a smithy and a coal merchant's yard. Grandpa Cook was a strong and gentle farm worker with the most beautiful voice that would charm the rowdies in a pub of a Saturday night. I had two of the most loving Grandpas you could imagine. Here are a few lines about them in a little poem which is simply called "Grandpas".

GRANDPAS

In the sunbaked thirties
We lived with Grandpa, while his Army son
Served the King in foreign climes.
This Grandpa kept the One Bell inn.
He was a comfortable brown –
His walnut face, his cords,
His knee-length riding boots, a relic from
His Army years or from his days as groom.

At three years old I helped him in the bar,
Collecting lunch-time empties.
Broken glass and blood were features of my help,
And Mother quietly saying "No",
Yet proud of me for wanting to help out.

I'd chatter to the poachers and the ploughmen,
And watch the dark spittoon
With brass around the rim
Fill up and sometimes overspill.

I'd glance at the stuffed trout
Inside his case of glass,
And both of us would gaze
Upon the trickle on the floor.

A mile away another Grandpa lived,
His cottage small and bent
 Beside the Essex road.
The privy half a mile away
Beyond the runner beans,
Where spiders lurked with hairy legs.

Nearby, the coalman Moy
Displayed his wares
In his front yard.
We climbed his hills of coal,
The black slack rasping down,
Invading boots and shoes
And smudging skin and clothes,

Then, tired of this black hour
And suddenly aware
Of retribution due,
We stood in awe inside the smithy,
Tolerated there by Grandpa's friend
To watch the black-red-white-red-black
Of iron, hear the clang and hiss,
And savour that sweet fragrance,
The new-mown hay of burning hoof.

Ah, God, the childish memories!

And meeting Grandpa on his way from work,
Leading his horse, his Suffolk Punch,
An Eiffel Tower in height above the road,
And being slung by Grandpa,
Legs athwart an acre of the beast's warm flesh.

Part 4: IN MORE SERIOUS VEIN

And that was Grandpa Cook,
Who sat with us upon the back door stoop,
Preparing Grandma's veg
While singing to his God and to the world
His repertoire of hymns and Irish songs.

The COMPLETE WIT & WHIMSEY

On Dad's return to England he was posted to Bulford, a garrison in Wiltshire, where we joined him. There we remained until war broke out, and it was there that I received my first taste of education.

A MILITARY EDUCATION

When I was four, an Army brat,
I lived in Bulford Barracks, Wilts
And started school.

My Daddy was a soldier.
He learned to fight.
I learned to write.
I also learned to read
And I learned History, which was all about cavemen
And Geography, which was all about the
British Empire,
The bits of the world that were pink,
And which we were proud of.
We were in charge of the British Empire
And our job
Was to teach all the black people about Jesus and to stop them
Eating each other.
That was important. I was also important
Because my birthday was on Empire Day
And all the soldiers paraded for me
And marched with bands.

Even though Daddy seemed cross most of the time
And liked to shout at Mother, my brother and me,
It was quite good fun having a Daddy in the Army
Because of all the troops
Marching, and firing on the butts
And having tattoos with motorbikes going up ramps
And through fiery hoops.
They were very good at being soldiers. You could tell.
They did it well
And my Daddy was one of them.
Some soldiers even wore kilts
In Bulford Barracks, Wilts.

Part 4: IN MORE SERIOUS VEIN

But suddenly one day, two years later,
After I became six,
The teacher gave us all a cardboard box
And said we were at war,
And a wicked country called Germany
Might try to kill us all with gas,
So we had to learn how to stop that
By wearing our gas-mask,
Which was inside the cardboard box.
We didn't want to die
So we looked at our teacher,
Every feature
Concentrated.

Teacher said *"Now quiet, don't shout,*
Slowly take your gas-masks out.
Put the boxes in your laps
And place your thumbs inside the straps.

Now pull the mask up on your chin
And wiggle it until it's in.
Now pull the straps behind your head
And that should do it", teacher said.

Gas-mask drill was fun
(As it was meant to be)
Because when you breathed out,
The breath made its way out the rubber sides
With a rude noise.
That made us all laugh, both girls and boys,
Which made noises even ruder.
And so on.
But your face got sweaty
And the perspex eye-piece soon steamed up,
So it wasn't all fun.
But we did learn how not to die through gas
And we didn't mind now about being at war.
We would win, anyway, because the people I lived with
Were very good
At being soldiers.

The COMPLETE WIT & WHIMSEY

Soon Daddy went away to France.
We didn't stay much longer in Bulford Barracks, Wilts.
The Army sent us to East Kent

To be nearer the war.

Just before Christmas 1939, the Army moved us to northeast Kent to an area known as the Isle of Thanet, while my father joined the British Expeditionary Force in France. We were assigned a billet in Cliftonville, the posh end of Margate – if there is a posh end. After a very severe winter, and with the threat of invasion looming, we were evacuated from there at the end of May – the time of Dunkirk. This poem covers that part of 1940.

FIRST GLIMPSE OF WAR

Winter 1940 was the worst
In living memory.
We lived in Thanet
Where the sea froze.
Trains were clogged in drifts
And only the bravest tractors
Reached the livestock.

Down on the beach
Smoke from Woodbines mingled with
Steaming breath
As soldiers pegged barbed-wire onto the beach
To stop an invasion.
Mines from the Channel
Were washed up daily.
The mine-detector plane from Manston,
Hoop deployed,
Patrolled the sea.
We fancied we saw periscopes,
But so did all the boys.

School was unlike school had been
In Army camps.
Here, many children spoke no English.
Most were shy and cautious.
We heard their fathers had escaped the Germans

Part 4: IN MORE SERIOUS VEIN

To join the RAF
And had got their families out with them.
We knew then that they were brave
And we shared our sweets with them.

Air-raid practice came at night
Once or twice a week.
Then it was under the table.
There were no shelters yet.
We knew it was all pretend then,
But one day, perhaps soon, it would be for real.

Around mid-May we heard the war.
Ominous rumblings, fainter than the most distant
    thunderstorm,
Were felt rather than heard,
But real enough for all that.
Everyone sensed them –
The guns on the mainland,
Pulsing tremors through the body.

The end of May
Saw utter chaos:
One hundred thousand troops
Plucked from Dunkirk were landed
At Margate, Ramsgate, Broadstairs, too,
While all the schools in Thanet also left,
Evacuated to a child.

On railway stations
Heaving throngs of bodies big and small
Vied for standing space,
Some khaki-clad, white-faced and bandaged,
Some tiny, scrubbed and labelled, clutching
Fish-paste sandwiches and teddy bears.

The COMPLETE WIT & WHIMSEY

Here is another instalment in my childhood wartime memories. We kept moving around the South of England, at the Army's behest, spending many nights under the table or in shelters.

AIR RAID SCHOLARS

The Army in its wisdom put us here,
Near Bletchley, where my father worked.
Air raid warnings tired us every night
For we were in the area, they said,
For notice of all threats to London Town,
Home Counties or the Midlands –
The busy southern catchment area.

We sheltered under table flaps,
With comics and a torch,
Until that magic day
The Anderson arrived
For planting in the garden,
A sturdy, corrugated den
Made more secure by tons of soil
Heaped on the bolted chunks of roof.
And made more lovely by the salvias
Planted in that soil.
Ours was deemed
The finest in the road:
So take that, Goering!

We were not bombed much,
Though once the rec. was strafed
In daylight hours.
At school, most were evacuees
Of some sort or another.
Nearly all were sent from London.
We were different:
We were Army.
It seemed a curious place to send
Those London children to,
With air raid warnings every night.
But all was relative.
London parents claimed their brood
Upon a lull perceived at home.

"Just one house in our street was hit all week.
So I'll take Jimmy home till it gets bad again."

This made for very interesting school,
Attendance- tariff based on air raids:
One air raid warning with the sleep foregone
Sanctioned late arrival at the school.
Two air raid warnings usually allowed
Attendance only in the afternoon.
But anyone could go in all the time
If they felt able.

Most days we went,
Though loss of sleep was cruel:
It led to crusty eyes
Which bled when picked at with a nail.

No lessons could be planned, with half a
    school at home,
While others came and went to London
    on parental whim.
Remnant classes came together,
Brought together, taught together
In the self same room.
Seven-year-olds looped letters and the
    twelve-year-olds learnt French,
While those of fourteen lisped a
    Shakespeare play –
Or so the theory went.

I know a boy, then seven, ears agog, who
    feasted on
Precocious increments
Of French and Shakespeare,

    Courtesy of air raids.

Part 4: IN MORE SERIOUS VEIN

By 1942, after several moves around the South of England and numerous air-raids, we were finally billeted by the Army in a small town in the West Riding of Yorkshire, while Dad went out of our lives for the next three years. We were much safer in Yorkshire than in the South, but I soon found that some of the children had real problems. They were clothed literally in rags, the boys often with their bare buttocks showing. Some wore no socks, even in winter. Many had faces painted purple, denoting impetigo under treatment. If their Dads weren't away in the Forces, they were working down the pit or in one of the many mills, mostly processing wool waste (or 'shoddy' as it was known) for recycling as cloth. Wages were pathetically small, shifts were long and work went on around the clock. Winters were dark, bleak and wet. Our billet was near the pit and one of the mills. This poem is called "Shift Workers".

SHIFT-WORKERS

I remember them,
On damp November mornings
Making for the pit.
The hooter went at seven.
They ambled down the road
In clusters, in the drizzle,
Clogs clattering on the cobbles
Below my window,
The smoke from their fags rising in their
    chatter
To show up yellow in the dim, puttering
    gaslight,
Shaded down for wartime.
I shivered, glad of another half-hour
In a warm bed
In a two-room billet
In a little Yorkshire town.

I remember the others, too,
Following the miners,
The men bound for the mill.
Their hooter went at seven-thirty,
Same clogs on cobbles,
Same fags, same chatter, same smoke
Rising to the dim, downward light,
Same November morning.

There were mill girls, too,
With fags and shawls and headscarves.
When I heard them giggling, I knew
It was time for me to get up
Out of my warm bed
In our two-room billet
In a little Yorkshire town.

I remember after school
We had our tea of wartime rations,
Played outside, then watched the lamp-lighter
Riding the cobbles of Tattersfield Street
    with his pole
Extended like a lance for jousting,
Propping his bike against the post
And setting the mantle puttering,
    puttering.
Now we played beneath this rare,
    dimmed gas-lamp
Until called in
Around the change of shift:
More clogs on cobbles,
A two-way stream now,
Jaundiced air with fag-smoke and chatter
Near our two-room billet
In a little Yorkshire town.

The COMPLETE WIT & WHIMSEY

This poem follows on logically from my wartime poems. The older I get, the more I find myself reminiscing about the past, not only my time at school, much of which was during the war, but the immediate post-war years with their Town Hall or Youth Club dances. And the people I seem to remember the most in those years were the girls in my life. So here is a little tribute to them.

GIRLS I REMEMBER

I remember when girls were the ones who had long hair
And danced backwards.
They lined up along the wall
And looked gorgeous in those posh frocks they wore
Before jeans had crossed the Atlantic
And girls still had legs made of flesh.

I remember, too, when I helped girls on the bus
With their French homework,
Back in the days when they wore
Navy-blue knickers they could tuck their hem into
For PE or hockey.
(The Convent girls wore bottle-green ones
And said they had to stand on a mirror
To prove it to Sister.)
Hankies and other things were secreted
In a mysterious pocket
Just above the elastic in the leg.

I remember, even earlier,
When the siren sounded and we were ushered
In obedient crocodiles
To the school shelter, dim, damp and dripping,
All puddles, sharp concrete and hard seats.

When the sky was full of the drone of Dorniers
And dull thumps caused things to tremble,
The teachers made us sing.
Then a little hand would seek my own as we sat there, afraid
And softly singing.
She was my first girl-friend.
And I can't remember her name.

Part 4: IN MORE SERIOUS VEIN

But I met another girl
And we married over fifty years ago.
Until then I had found no-one to share fear and excitement with
Since the air raids.

The COMPLETE WIT & WHIMSEY

Over the years, I've visited several elderly relatives in care homes, where it's easy to get the impression that the residents, especially the very elderly, sit still and stare ahead of them. I'm sure these homes can be a little frightening to these old folk, though the carers seem to be a special breed. The ones I've met are lovely people. Here is a poem that will, I hope, evoke these residential homes, as we follow a very old man through his day.

THERE WAS A TIME

The old man did as he was told:
He lived his life amid the clocks.
They ordered everything he did:
They moved him on from box to box.
They told him when to leave his bed
And when the carer, bearing towels,
Was due to come to help him bath
Or sit him down to move his bowels.
They told him when a meal was due
And when to take his fifteen pills
That kept him ticking on and on,
Protecting him from fifteen ills.

The clocks would tell him when to sit
And stare upon the patterned wall.
He was expected to do this
Not all the time, but nearly all.
Sometimes his weeping eyes would stray
Beyond the steamy window's frame,
Where dimly he would see a field,
A ball, some boys, a breathless game.
There was a time when he'd done that,
About five hundred years ago,
When he was strong in arm and lung,
When he could run and kick and throw

Sometimes the carer would be Grace,
The big girl with the grown-up boys.
He loved her sunny, chocolate face
Her every movement stamped with poise.
There was a time girls smiled at him,
About five hundred years ago,
And he would softly talk to them,
Desired them all, and let them know.
He'd tell Grace "You can bath me now
Provided I can bath you after."
She'd gently say "You dirty man."
And stroke his head amid the laughter.

His days had been reduced to rote
His actions all habitual:
Washing, eating, potty time,
A life-sustaining, sterile ritual.
And staring with unending gaze
Upon that badly-papered wall:
Those bloody roses, pink and blurred.
He hated them, he loathed them all.
There was a time his friends stopped by,
There was a time his children came,
But now his visitors stayed home,
Embarrassed at his failing frame.

His efforts to communicate
Might find him short of breath and
    mumbling.
His clothes the time of life he'd reached:
His velcro years, the age of fumbling.
And yet, and yet, he had his mind
And memories that would always last:
He now loved girls of long ago
And fought the battles of the past.
The clocks might show him when to do
The things with which he had to cope,
But in his mind were other times –
Those times of conquest and of hope!

Part 4: IN MORE SERIOUS VEIN

Here's another poem about a very old man. I won't tell you what his problem is. Perhaps you can guess. All I will say is that he's very, very frightened.

ORDEAL

He stared, terrified. There were three of them.
One was a man in white.
There was a woman in a sort of uniform.
Blue.
And another woman, with thick arms,
In a flowery thing.

"Well?"
Panic seized him.
They wanted an answer.
But he had none.
He looked wildly around him,
As if searching for a means of escape.
The three heads leant closer to him.
"Well?" Louder this time.
"Have you decided?"

He sensed hostility,
But he wouldn't let them intimidate him.
He'd been a soldier once.
He'd look them straight in the eye.
He felt better now, stronger.

He cleared his throat,
Glared at each of them in turn
And, in a quavering squeak
said "That one".

The three of them looked at each other.
"There was no doubt about it"
Said the man in white.
"I agree" said the woman in a sort of uniform.
Blue.
"So do I" said the other woman, with thick arms,
In a flowery thing.

"He definitely pointed to the Bakewell Tart."

The COMPLETE WIT & WHIMSEY

I first wrote this poem in 1968 when we lived in Silver Spring, Maryland. The climate there is sub-tropical and the summers are extremely hot. Throughout July and August, the humidity is very high and this combination of heat and humidity generates the most dramatic thunderstorms virtually every day some time between 5 pm and 7 pm. In the poem I compare the storm to a bully preying on the weak. Since the first draft, I have tinkered a little with the wording, but the poem remains very largely as it was first written.

SUMMER STORM: MARYLAND

Dark broods the distance, murmur turns to growl
And lingers long and low, begets another.
Crooning mother
Comforts child, wide-eyed with silent fear.

Now seething cumulus teems up, and jaundiced murk
Encompasses three quarters of the sky.
Blind darts begin to stab the sickly gloom.
With boom
And bombast blunders in the bully,
Grumbling from on high
To spit his venom on the ground below:
Ring-ding upon the hard, black asphalt loud,
Pelting it with water-pebbles plucked
From pressure-punctured cloud,
While tousled trees bend passive to their fate.
Frail, plunder'd flowers cower homage to the Great,
And birds their song abate.

Sleek limousines awash whisk, hissing by,
Enamelled lustre mirrored in the wet,
And peering drivers seek to steer their course,
Bemused by wipers lurching fast, but yet
Unable to contain the streaming force.

Part 4: IN MORE SERIOUS VEIN

For sixteen sodden minutes Earth is soaked,
Then all is still. And shafts of gold and silver
Search the land, inspect the legacy
Of steaming pools, exhausted, limping bowers
And convalescent flowers,
While, proud of conquests made this day,
The bully slinks away
With misconceived illusion he is King,

- Yet birds now sing.

And child escapes from mother's arms,
His whimpering stilled,
His body filled
With love and confidence.

The tender power of parent will surpass
The whims of elements unleashed.

Storm break, child fear,
Mother love – God's panacea.

The COMPLETE WIT & WHIMSEY

I wrote this poem in 1967 before our twins, Sue and Helen, were born. We drove from Silver Spring, Maryland, to South Carolina and stayed near Myrtle Beach. On the way down, we passed through some very turbulent weather and saw some pretty squalid shacks where the black people lived. The violent weather, with tornados never far away, somehow seemed to accentuate the extreme poverty we noticed. My original words are retained: 'Negro' was the accepted way of referring to black people in those days.

THE BEACH

Palm trees and a white, clean shore.
The moon rides up, with restless silver prints the sea.
Suddenly
Three Negro boys on bicycles race o'er the sand.
These cannot be
Of those that live in abject misery
In squalid, crumbling shacks
And live from hand to mouth.
Driving South
We saw many such as they
In this land of wealth and claimed equality.

This beach is where the English met a Spanish force.
The English won, of course.
But who cares?
Their heirs
Established Charleston and the towns around.
History records
The carefree life of English lords
In Carolina, when there were
No bicycles as toys

For little Negro boys.

Part 4: IN MORE SERIOUS VEIN

I'm fascinated by the ancient history of Winchcombe, my home town in the north Cotswolds, and of the surrounding area. All about us is evidence of Roman occupation, with remnants of the villas occupied not only by Romans themselves, but by the Romano-Britons, the Celtic chiefs who adopted their lifestyle. There is a ruined villa deep in Spoonley Wood near Winchcombe, totally uncared for, because there are so many of them, and other villas better preserved command most of the attention and the money for their upkeep as tourist attractions. But long before the Romans, hunter-gatherers from the mainland of what became Europe were here, gradually evolving into the first farmers and building elaborate burial monuments, such as Belas Knapp, a long barrow high up on the Cotswold escarpment above Winchcombe. Here is a poem that seeks to encapsulate all these periods and take us back to our roots.

GENERATIONS

A long, damp hike has brought us here
Through fields of shifting sheep.

Now deep in Spoonley Wood
We gaze in wonder at the remnant walls.

The spattered lichen and the binding moss
Preserve the evidence of ancient habitation.

We tread among the scattered roofing slates,
The nail-holes crafted out
Some eighteen hundred years ago,
Yet still appearing fresh.

In one damp corner empty fertilizer bags
Held down by stones
Provide a token preservation for a bathroom's rich mosaic,
Celtic-patterned, whorled and crossed.
And there a pit, now choked with crowded nettles
Betrays a relic hypocaust.

These Britons kept their Celtic rule,
Their ancient tribal heritage.
They bargained with their Latin lords:
They said "We'll lay aside our swords,
We'll save you work, we'll rule our hordes.

Just let us live like you."
And so it was.

They farmed, they hunted,
Wed, gave birth and died.

They sometimes made the steep ascent
Through fields of shifting sheep
To Belas Knapp
To gaze in wonder at the ancient tomb,
Knew its sanctity, sensed antiquity,
But would not know,
Nor would their Latin lords,
That it was crafted
Nigh four thousand years before
When refugees from Celtic war,
Their misty ancestors, fled here
To burn the wildwood, clear the scarp
Put sheep to pasture
And close wild cattle in
With dry-stone walls.

They it was who pioneered the art,
Contrived to interlace the limestone slates,
And with the self-same skill
Worked piece with piece and slowly formed a barrow
For their fathers' bones,
And topped it overall with soil,
Till there it stood, like some vast earthen carapace.

They daily hiked from hut to tomb
Through flocks of shifting sheep
Their labours to perform.
And, weary from an honest day's endeavour,
Would sit around their tribal fire
Where, drunk with foaming juice from rotting apples,
They told fables from their ancient lore
Of missions to this close and fruitful hunting ground
Across a sunken bridge of frozen marsh,
Before the ice withdrew and spawned an isle.

And we descend from these.

Part 4: IN MORE SERIOUS VEIN

I wrote this in 1999 as Winchcombe's Millennium poem. It is included in the Millennium Book, which I edited and which, incredibly, sold nearly 2,000 copies in a town of fewer than 5,000 people. Two reprints were necessary. The poem attempts to encapsulate some 10,000 years of Man's settlement in and around the place we now call Winchcombe. The famous Parish church with its golden cockerel naturally gets a mention.

HOME

Three hundred generations back
Came hunters up the Cotswold track.
They tamed the wildwood, cleared a belt,
To fatten stock and scatter spelt.
They lugged the limestone from the loam
And settled there. And called it home.

For untold years, with tribal pride
They farmed, they fought, they loved, they died.
Invaders came and foreign yoke
Subdued these simple Celtic folk,
Until the armies sailed for Rome
And left them to their Cotswold home.

The Saxons found the Cotswold trail
And planted Winchcombe in a vale.
Their pagan ways they sacrificed
When Mercia bent the knee to Christ.
Then Normans came with Doomsday tome
And counted every Winchcombe home.

But famine, plague, revolt and strife
Dealt mortal blows to Winchcombe life.
Then wealth returned. In field and fold
Fine fleeces grew. Or on the wold
Men pastured flocks and let them roam
And multiply and make their home.

Now see the buzzards up on high
Sail graceful spirals in the sky.
They surely know, while gazing down
Upon the green that girds the town,
That golden cock with crimson comb
Will guide us to our Winchcombe home.

The COMPLETE WIT & WHIMSEY

Behind the main street that runs through Winchcombe are the Back Fields, a group of fields with public right of way, which still show signs of the ridge and furrow land allocation of feudal times in the 11th Century. The tiny River Isbourne runs alongside. The views of the town itself and the hills in the opposite direction are among the finest in the Cotswolds. I often walk this way into the town.

THE BACK FIELDS

As long as God permits me strength
I'll walk the Back Fields path
And savour it throughout its length.
I'll loiter by the Isbourne's flow
To watch the trout patrol below
And mallards at their bath.

I'll point my gaze to Stancombe Hill,
Where sheep, contented, drift,
Calling, grazing at their will.
And there, above the forest dense
The buzzards' vigil is intense
For tell-tale stir or shift.

In hotch-potch order up the rise
The village houses stand.
Their random pattern draws the eyes.
Our ancient stock, their tongues long stilled
Regarded them, the while they tilled
The undulating land.

The corrugations of the soil
Lie row by honest row –
The measure of a worker's toil.
To feed his family he was proud,
His ridge and furrow neatly ploughed,
A thousand years ago.

The soil remains, the men are gone.
What joys, what burdens theirs?
The plough they placed their hand upon
Is long since gone, for go it must,
The yoke, the share, reduced to dust
And we walk here, their heirs.

Part 4: IN MORE SERIOUS VEIN

Deep in the Cotswolds lie the ruins of Hailes Abbey, a Cistercian monastery, and one of the many victims of Henry VIII's policy to dissolve all religious institutions except Parish churches, following the Pope's refusal to recognise the legitimacy of his divorce from Catherine of Aragon and marriage to Anne Boleyn. Hailes was invaded and its destruction set in motion on Christmas Day 1539. Some poets have written of the beauty of the ruins of these religious houses and of the noble thoughts they inspire. By contrast, I tend to feel sorrow and anger.

HAILES ABBEY

If I were to write a poem about a ruined abbey,
I would not find cold, graceful relics in a Cotswold vale
A source of peace and purity, as some have done.

The setting, so tranquil, so swathed in beauty
Is in stark contrast to the reality of what I see,
When images of plunder, unbidden, obtrude.

If I were to write a poem about a ruined abbey
I would see thoughtful Cistercians preparing their chapel for the Nativity
Or scurrying to the domestic bidding of Father Abbot.

Someone would have checked their supplies of meat and the soil's produce
Gleaned from the bountiful slopes of Hailes and Farmcote
And shared with the villagers. Someone always did.

All is ready. Brother Peter is designated to celebrate Mass
For the villagers in their own little church near the abbey –
Their familiar stone sanctuary with hunting scenes adorning the stucco.

"What's that noise, Brother Peter? Christmas Day in the abbey?
Tumultuous celebration?" Nay. 'Tis Cromwell with two hundred of horse,
Smashing, stealing, beating all that moves, or is still.

"Strip the lead from the roofs, lads, then put to fire!"
The brothers flee, shivering, to the woods, those left alive.
The villagers stand white-faced.

The COMPLETE WIT & WHIMSEY

If I were to write a poem about a ruined abbey
I would think of a monarch with fevered loins
Taking a second spouse and wreaking vengeance on those who
    disapproved.

I would not find cold, graceful relics in a Cotswold vale
A source of peace and purity, as some have done,
When images of plunder, unbidden, obtrude.

Part 4: IN MORE SERIOUS VEIN

I sometimes write verse for family occasions and even sad events can be the occasion for a poem. And the poem itself does not necessarily have to be sad or, worse still, mawkish. There's room for a light touch as long as the poem is written with genuine affection. My mother, was a wonderful person, who had battled with severe deafness from the age of about 50. In all that time she never could master the use of a hearing aid, and used to fasten the battery bit to her bra, because it seemed to fall off anywhere else she wore it. This meant undoing her blouse to hold a conversation. She claimed the hearing aids never worked properly. She brought up 3 children in the war while Dad was away, protecting us from the bombing and sacrificing her own rations to feed us. She used to say the silliest things, quite unconsciously. When I was a hungry teenager, always looking around for something to eat, she once said to me "Don't eat all those apples. They don't grow on trees, you know!" When she died in 1997, housebound with arthritis, and, of course, stone deaf for many years, I felt I had to pay a short poetic tribute to her at the funeral. The little poem I wrote is called "The Deaf Shall Hear."

THE DEAF SHALL HEAR

She's gone, God bless her lonely soul,
She's gone to final rest,
To where the Lord has made a place
For those He loves the best,
Where blind will see and deaf will hear
And lame will walk again,
Where Death will have no victory
And dear ones feel no pain.

And when they open Heaven's gate
She'll stand there unafraid
And tell them that it didn't work,
That stupid hearing aid.
They'll smile and take her by the hand
And then - you mark my words -
She'll hear the choirs of Heaven
And the sweet celestial birds.

She's happy now, God bless her,
She's happy at the loss
Of that twilight world of silence
That was her mortal cross.
How could she be so cheerful
All those years she never heard
The chattering of children
Or the singing of a bird?

Here is a short poem based on something that happened in church on a November morning. It made such an impact on me that I sat down as soon as I got home, and wrote these few lines.

WHY?

Remembrance Sunday. There we sat
In suits. Some women wore a hat.
A sea of poppies, faces white
Or yellowed from a candle's light.

The Minister spoke movingly:
He asked us all the question 'Why?'
That murder in the mud of France,
Why did those thousands have to die?
And why were all those families killed
When planes rained slaughter from the sky?
'Why' said the Minister again,
'Why did these people have to die?'

He called a minute's silence then,
A time for prayer and quiet reflection
And pondering the question 'Why?'
We sat in solemn introspection.
The seconds crept in utter quiet,
There was no sigh, no whispered word,
Then suddenly with urgent voice
A loud and plaintive sound was heard.
From somewhere at the back of church
We heard a tiny baby cry

And knew at once the right reply –
The answer to the question 'Why?'

Part 4: IN MORE SERIOUS VEIN

A few years ago I was invited by the local press to write them a poem about Christmas in Cheltenham, because they had very kindly publicised one of my books of poetry. So I strolled about Cheltenham, watching and listening. The magic clock in the Regent Arcade with the snake and the mouse attracted its usual crowd of toddlers. I even peered through school and office windows. So here we are - a poem about Christmas in Cheltenham, called "Aspects of Advent".

ASPECTS OF ADVENT

See the glare and shadow blending
As the crowds forever throng,
Never-ending, ever-spending,
Listening to the Christmas song
From the brave Salvation Army
Fighting in the rain the fight:
Rousing, joyful "Herald Angels",
Soft and peaceful "Flocks by Night".

See the busy schools rehearsing
Breathless children for the stage:
Five and twenty little Josephs,
Marys, too, of tender age.
See the happy office parties -
Everybody knows the drill:
Bosses all beam down benignly,
Typing pool is dressed to kill.

See the helpful, friendly copper
Stroll about the pavements bright.
See the tiny Christmas shopper
Clutching Mother's glove so tight.
Santa was a revelation:
Will he really find my house?
Looks at clock with trepidation:
Will the big snake eat the mouse?

See the homeless in the doorways
Seeking shelter and a bite.
See the strangers offer mangers,
Soup and blanket for the night.
Selfless band of benefactors,
Mrs Jones and Mr Brown,
Oh, little town of Cheltenham
Your God is surely smiling down.

The COMPLETE WIT & WHIMSEY

In a world torn in many parts by war and where even the pace of modern living presents a challenge, it is a comfort to hold fast to those things that mean most to us and bring us peace – the beauties of nature, a sense of community and perhaps, above all, our home and our loved ones. Many things contribute to that feeling of peace and well-being we need to turn to. Here are a few thoughts of my own in a poem which is simply called "Peace".

PEACE

Peace is the drowsy, bee-warm hum round a hammock's lazy sway
And the distant drone as a lawn is mown in the balm of a sun-blest day.
Peace is the cold, clear call of the owls that I hear from a winter's bed,
And the sigh of the sycamores down the lane as a summer's growth is shed.
Peace is the urgent surge of surf and the backwash beat from the sand,
And the sharp-etched white of sails in flight as they tackle the tack to land.
Peace is the sound of a Sunday crowd as they pray to their Lord in song,
And the smile and the nod from the children of God when the Brigadier gets it wrong.
Peace is the shout as the school pours out to the playground's push and shove,
And the smile in the eye of the passers by who spy with pride and love.

Peace is the hearth that I sit beside, and the smile that you smile at me,
And the squeeze of your hand and the smell of your hair
  - and the warm, shared tea.

Part 4: IN MORE SERIOUS VEIN

These gentle little sonnets speak for themselves.

GARDEN SONNETS

I THE SLUG

He prompts a universal "Ugh!"
But I've affection for the slug.
He's not aggressive, doesn't fight,
And never makes a noise at night.
He doesn't worry if he's late:
His pace through life is quite sedate.
Sophistication he may lack,
But seldom has a heart attack.
Above all this, I love the slug
Because he makes me feel so smug:
He deigns to rate my modest crops
As fodder fitting for his chops!

He slides his way between my rows,
Dispensing silver as he goes.

II THE WORM

As you walk on *terra firma*,
'Neath the surface lurks a worm: a
Friend to man, who toils and toils
To penetrate the densest soils,
And though designed through life to crawl
His industry should shame us all.
And yet his lot in life is but
To end up in a thrush's gut,
Or else be riven by the blade
Of misdirected hoe or spade.
Perhaps we ought to bear in mind
The parallel within mankind:

That predators are out to feed
On those who toil but pay no heed.

III THE ANT

When conversation turns to ants
I tend to take a neutral stance.
I think they're at their very best
When somebody disturbs their nest.
Some people say they just can't stand 'em
(Think they mill around at random):
But this activity disguises
Trained reaction to a crisis,
As all respond on tiny legs
To leader's call "Secure the eggs!"
Now, creatures who their young protect
Deserve a good deal of respect.

But as to liking them - that's harder,
Especially when they're in my larder.

IV THE WOODLOUSE

I've never really understood
Why woodlice have a yen for wood:
They're born there, live there, laugh and cry there,
Mate, and ultimately die there.
Wood is home and wood is bed.
It also serves as daily bread:
At mealtimes see the woodlouse reach
For chips of oak or ash or beech.
When courting, woodlouse suitor meets a
Woodlouse girl for poplar pizza,
Or then, up-market they might dine
On elm supreme, *brochettes* of pine.

Live on, secure in larch or willow,
You teeny-weeny armadillo.

V THE HONEY BEE

The honey bee spends all his hours
Popping in and out of flowers
Or illustrating geography
By means of choreography.
He dances to convey the sector
Where he found a fund of nectar:
Bearing, distance, colour, number,
Foxtrot, quickstep, waltz and rumba.
But what a thankless life he lives:
Unstintingly his time he gives,
And gets ignored by queen and drones,
But yet he never ever moans.

To crown it all (it can't be funny)
Along comes man and steals his honey

VI THE CENTIPEDE

I've seldom felt a pressing need
To envy Mr Centipede:
He cannot breathe, he cannot eat
Without considering his feet.
They rule his life, his every deed,
His love for fellow centipede.
One thing I'm grateful to have missed -
The bill from his chiropodist:
I know I'd be forever broke -
Five hundred toenails are no joke.
And if he has some inflamation,
What's his system of notation?

"Oh, Doc, my leg feels sort of tight -
That's forty-seven on the right."

VII THE SPIDER

Many people can't abide a
Harmless, inoffensive spider.
I've often saved a certain wife
From deadly peril to her life
By taking down the garden path
Spiders that invade her bath:
It's lucky that in our abode
Not everyone's arachnophobe.
I'm only sorry I can't save
The poor male spider from his grave,
Because upon their honeymoon
The female strikes a note of gloom:

Immediately they consummate
That's what she does - consume her mate!

VIII THE LADYBIRD

I'd like to say a little word
In favour of the ladybird.
She's quite the prettiest of things
She seldom bites and never stings.
She truly is the gardener's friend
By driving aphids round the bend
(For aphids are her favoured diet,
Disgusting food - you want to try it!)
So treat her with a velvet glove:
Talk to her and call her "love".
And get acquainted with the date
On which she plans to hibernate.

Then gently pat her on the head
And offer her the garden shed.

Part 4: IN MORE SERIOUS VEIN

IX THE BUTTERFLY

It only takes a hint of Spring
Ere butterflies are on the wing.
Their task: to feed, then procreate,
First find your food, then find a mate.
The clever ones lurk on wisterias
Looking sexy and mysterious,
But most seek out a venue cuddlier,
So congregate upon a buddleia,
And, when a pair say "I love you",
They leap aloft and then pursue
Their courtship lepidopteral
With movements helicopteral.

Do caterpillars gaze in dread?
Does fear of flying fill each head?

The COMPLETE WIT & WHIMSEY

INDEX TO FIRST LINES (EXCLUDING LIMERICKS)

A Bridge-playing lady called Claire	107
A funny thing I've found with sneezes	84
After God created man	10
A furry brown creature popped out of his hole	60
A long, damp hike has brought us here	135
A million miles above the skies	32
Another day in Paradise	8
As I sat in a country inn	91
As long as God permits me strength	138
As Miss Muffet sat eating her porridge	81
As you walk on *terra firma*	145
Aunt Ethel, on the Tour Eiffel	59
A whirlwind take you, Michael Fish	58
Boy Blue oft neglected his sheep	81
"Can I become famous in the literary world?"	85
Convinced he was well out of sight	81
Dark broods the distance, murmur turns to growl	132
Dewi Morgan earned his keep	16
Forgive me if I sound downcast	79
Fosdyke of the FCO	45
Geoffrey Peters, Bridge fanatic	105
Georgie Porgie, with lecherous leers	81
Gordon Brown	118
Hail to thee, BlitheSpirit	118
Hark while this tale I now unfold	38
He prompts a universal "Ugh!"	145
He stared, terrified. There were three of them	131
I cut myself while shaving	55
I'd like to get to Heaven	14
I'd like to say a little word	146
If I were to write a poem about a ruined abbey	139
If you develop diabetes	83
I have a little Satnav	90
I like to sit and reminisce	68
I must go down to the sea again	118
In a courtroom one day	81
In a mansion somewhat grotty	34
In days of old, so we are told	66
In mediæval times, they say	41
In my garden, unannounced	73

INDEX TO FIRST LINES

In Picardy, there stands a town	28
In the annals of our land	88
In the claustrophobic gloom	18
In Xanadu did Kubla Khan	118
I remember them	127
I remember when girls were the ones who had long hair	128
It only takes a hint of Spring	147
I've never really understood	145
I've seldom felt a pressing need	146
Lady Amanda Dalrymple	101
Little Arthur, with a gun	59
"Lucy darling," said her mother	59
Many people can't abide a	146
Mother Hubbard, in tears, shook her head	81
Mrs Spenser-Smythe looks down	15
My love – you're like an unmade bed	76
Near the hot Kalahari	69
Now Pedro was a pussy-cat	80
Oh, children are a wond'rous gift	82
"Oh, daughter dear," her mother said	97
Oh, dear Miss Phillips, spare a thought	53
Oh, earwigs they love to watch football	84
Oh, green, pretentious bowl of slime	86
Oh, have you heard of Paddy	99
Oh, they talks of it in Naafi's	20
Oh, what a naughty lady: she'd played that trick before	94
Oh, wise of mind and round of rump	107
On holiday in Cairo, Joe	59
On the wall Humpty Dumpty did say	81
On your sheet, so lily white	83
O, young Lochinvar is come out of the West	118
Paddy took his old car for a service	55
Palm trees and a white, clean shore	134
Peace is the drowsy, bee-warm hum round a hammock's lazy sway	144
Poor Jim sat dishevelled, his head on his knee	62
"Private Jones!" the Sergeant roared	59
Rab McTavish, piper braw	81
Rapunzel, Rapunzel, please let down your hair	82
Remembrance Sunday. There we sat	142
Ricardo – what a craftsman he	59
Said mother "Come and say hello to Vicar."	59
See the glare and shadow blending	143

The COMPLETE WIT & WHIMSEY

See the student in his teens	78
She's gone, God bless her lonely soul	141
Shhhh, shhhhh,shhhhh, shhhhh	65
Sluggy, sluggy, uggy-wuggy	75
Snow White, we think, was quite content	76
Some people love toads	84
Some Whitehall mandarins decreed	92
Some years ago, I understand	23
The Annual Convention	49
The Army in its wisdom put us here.	126
The curfew tolls the knell of parting day	118
The golfer had a super round	118
The honey bee spends all its hours	146
The old man did as he was told.	130
The policeman rushed into the ward	118
The Reverend Ian Paisley	118
The Sultan threw his wife into the sea	118
The Ugly Duckling's looking wan.	81
Three hundred generations back.	137
Three mice, with dark glasses and canes	102
To northern parts of Norfolk.	74
Tony Blair	118
Tricky the hands in the card room this evening.	108
'Twas mother's turn to host the Bridge	106
When Charlie cut the cable.	30
When conversation turns to ants	145
When festivals and holidays assail our sceptred isle	54
When Fred came out the Rose and Crown.	100
When I was at my Daddy's knee.	56
When I was four, an Army brat	122
When you're in a foreign land	71
Who is this Mr Phillips	87
Willie Winkie in nightshirt (no drawers)	81
Winter 1940 was the worst in living memory	124
"You sitta here," the artist said	67